A true story of life in the WAAF
during World War II

By

JEAN PATTERSON

First published 2011

ISBN 978-1-908115-00-3

A catalogue record for this book is available from the
British Library

Published by
Polstead Press

Front cover WAAF image by courtesy of the
R.A.F. Museum, Hendon
Cover design by Galleon Typesetting
Printed and bound by Polstead Press

Contents

Introduction		11
1	Deferred Service	13
2	Into Uniform	22
3	Postings and Parachutes	33
4	Remustering	42
5	Firewatching	52
6	Electrician II	65
7	Dried Egg and Foreigners	77
8	Kidbrooke	89
9	Absent Without Leave	108
10	Peace Reigns	127
11	At Last – Demob	135
Postscript		140

Service Trade...ACH/Tailoress...

R.A.F. Form 2150W

WOMEN'S AUXILIARY AIR FORCE

ENLISTMENT FOR DURATION OF THE PRESENT EMERGENCY

POSTPONEMENT OF CALLING UP FOR SERVICE

To No............ 2002076   Name...... Bailey J.

Address ...4 Rydal Walk, Nacton Estate
................Ipswich
....

Nearest Rly. Stn....Derby Road,.............

In connection with your enlistment in the Women's Auxiliary Air Force for service during the present emergency, you will be required to report for permanent service in accordance with the instructions contained in a notice to be issued to you by the Officer in Charge Records, Royal Air Force.

In the meantime you will remain on the Reserve and no pay or allowances will be issuable to you for the period during which you are not called up for permanent service. It is important therefore that you should not leave your present civil employment until you are required to report for service. Where practicable you will be notified ten days before the date on which you will be required to report.

The Air Officer in Charge Records, Royal Air Force, Ruislip, Middlesex, must be informed of any change of address, and any correspondence must quote your W.A.A.F. No. and name.

Station... London & S.E. Area Recruiting Unit

Date...... 25.6.41

For Air Officer i/c Records,
Royal Air Force.

(55316) Wt. 9233/68 200m 4/41 Hw. G.371

Foreword

Special thanks must go to the following:

Robert McMaster – Tenant Participation Manager, Ipswich Borough Council, whose assistance made this book possible.

Rev. R. Tobin who organised the words initially.

Huby Fairhead for the care given to my memorabilia at Flixton Aviation Museum.

All staff at Gainsborough Library, Ipswich, for all their help and encouragement.

Dedication

This book is dedicated to all wartime
W.A.A.F. wherever they may be.

Introduction

PREPARATIONS for war had been going on for some time. Hundreds of our boys had already been conscripted. Gas masks had been issued to the civilian population and lectures had been given on gas warfare. Air raid precautions were practised at work and in schools, and air raid shelters were already available. In spite of all this, the news that Britain was at war with Germany was a shock to most people.

I was 15 at the time – I had celebrated my birthday only three months before. While I knew nothing of war and its meaning, I couldn't help feeling a tingle of excitement.

My life to this point had been much the same as hundreds of other children. I had been born and brought up in the town of Ipswich, Suffolk, as had my father before me. My mother was born in Norwich, Norfolk, and came with her parents to live in Ipswich when she was seven.

I was the eldest of five children, my only brother being the youngest. My father was a bus driver and worked long hours to earn enough money to keep us all fed and clothed. My mother too was hardworking, always sewing and cooking and generally trying to make ends meet. Most of my young life was spent minding the children and helping with household chores.

At the age of 14 I left my secondary modern school and

went to work in the local tailoring factory. The factory was noted for its high quality suits, riding breeches and jackets. My job was hand sewing and finishing. We worked on the piecework system. I found this a good incentive and tried hard to earn more money than I did the week before. We worked a 52-hour week including Saturday mornings. This gave me my first taste of independence.

The entertainment of the time was the cinema. What little pocket money was left after paying my parents for my keep was spent almost entirely on seeing films. I'd go as often as three times a week if I could. I read, with fascination the life stories, scandals and anything connected with film stars. I made scrapbook after scrapbook of pictures cut out from the *Picturegoer* and *Film Weekly*. I even joined a picture postcard club and collected photographs of my favourite idols. These I cherished most dearly, and still do, although quite a lot of the names have long since been forgotten.

Popular music or dance music, as it was called then, was another of my interests. At work we would compete with each other to be the first to learn all the words of the latest hit tune. There was no 'Top Twenty' then but we were able to buy song sheets with all the words of the latest hits, but by the time these came on the market new songs had already taken their place. My parents thought these activities were a waste of time and money, and constantly told me so, but I just couldn't give them up or saw any reason to.

With all the films I went to see, it's no wonder I was a bit of a dreamer. I had a vivid imagination, which would some-times run riot, but never in my wildest dreams did I ever imagine that life would unfold itself in the way that it actually did.

Chapter 1

Deferred Service

THE first few weeks of the war went almost unnoticed and apart from the occasional 'Alert' everything appeared to be the same as usual. Everyone was saying the war would be over in six months.

The blackout was everyone's worry. The days were getting shorter with winter approaching and we had to get used to streets with no lights. Everyone carried a torch with the beam restricted according to regulations. Blackout material was on sale everywhere. This was bought and made into curtains so that not a glimmer of light could penetrate into the street. If there were so much as a chink of light showing, the air raid warden would knock on the door and ask for it to be smothered. Cars had special attachments made for the headlights to cut the beam to a minimum. Cyclists, too, were encouraged to have a good reflector on the rear of their cycles to enable them to be seen. Even with all this, people were still very cheerful and confident that everything was only temporary.

The factory where I worked was beginning to change over to making khaki uniforms. There was not so much hand sewing to be done on these, and for a while work was not so plentiful. As the civilian orders tapered off and the khaki came through we found ourselves waiting for work.

This went on for some weeks while adjustments were made on the factory floor. Government work gradually took over. Everyone then was working as hard as they could go. This didn't make a great deal of difference to me, and I was still happy in the job I was doing until . . .

One Monday morning I went into work as usual and was asked to move myself to the conveyor belt and to start working on a machine. I didn't like this idea at all, but had no choice. I wasn't afraid of the machine – I sometimes used a sewing machine at home – it was the thought of the conveyor belt that worried me. The girls on the 'belt' had always worked there and were used to feeding each other with work. I had always worked independently and the thought of having to keep pace with the experienced workers frightened me. Besides the fact that I had to leave the people I had grown to know so well and start all over again with strangers. I went under protest.

The first two days were a nightmare to me. Although, I was going as fast as I could go with this new job, I was still slow and work began to pile up. Those working on the garment after me were having to wait a while. They didn't say a word, I wished they had. They just looked at me and then at each other – I hated it. I went to see the foreman again to see if I could go back to my old job. His answer was negative. I didn't know quite what to do. I knew I couldn't stick at that job – it was like a treadmill. I had to do something.

I didn't go into work the next day or for the rest of the week. I told my parents I didn't feel well, and quite honestly, I didn't.

The following Monday I went to work again, but didn't

go back to the 'belt' but to my old job of hand sewing. The charge-hand asked me if I should be on the machine and I told her the machine job had only been temporary. I had done the job only to help out for a couple of days. She seemed to believe me and gave me some work. Not many minutes later the foreman came over and, once again, I was sent to work on the belt. I started off again on that dreaded job. It was no good, I just couldn't get used to it. Once more, I made up my mind to have words with the foreman. This time I would make it quite clear to him that I just couldn't continue to work on the machine.

I knocked timidly on his office door. He didn't call me in but came out to me. I only managed to get a couple of words across to him and as soon as he realised that I was objecting again, he started to shout at me. I could hear the machines behind me beginning to stop and the noise of the factory gradually lessened so that his voice could be heard all over the floor. He told me he had more to do than pander to my whims. Didn't I know there was a war on and the work had to be done. I was to go back to work and not cause any more trouble. If I wasn't satisfied I could collect my cards and leave. By this time I was in tears – not so much at what he said, but at the sheer humiliation of everyone else knowing as well. I was so embarrassed and everyone was looking at us and listening. If ever I wanted the floor to open up and swallow me, I did then. I asked for my cards.

I didn't feel so bad once I got home and told my parents. They backed me up and couldn't understand why such an issue had been made with one so young. I wasn't quite 16. I started looking for another job.

There was a new factory in town. It was a London firm

which had evacuated from the big city to Ipswich. They had renovated an old garage to suit their purposes – a Government contract to make khaki uniforms. I went there and got a job right away.

Once again they didn't want hand finishers so I took a job on a machine. This wasn't so bad because it was not on a conveyor belt. Here I worked on piecework again making battledress blouses. They were all cut out and ready to sew in bundles of a dozen. There were various sizes and it was a mad scramble to try to get the smaller sizes, giving us a fraction less machining to do yet earn the same money. We were paid four pence ha'penny (old money) for each blouse we completed, and more often than not we managed to make a dozen each day. There was a lot of overtime, at the same rate of course, and plenty of work. The forewoman in charge was a Cockney and had come to Ipswich with the firm. She spoke a language I had never heard before, cockney slang and swearing. It was all new to me and she blasphemed all day long. I soon learned, however, and many of the girls could give as good as they got!

Although the work wasn't strenuous, there was no relaxing. Trips to the loo were timed and counted. No chance of slipping off for 10 minutes respite. It was work, work, work. A strict eye was kept on absenteeism. The standard of work had to be constant and anything slapdash was literally thrown back with a string of abuse.

The forewoman passed the work, and she was not one to be trifled with. Chattering at work was almost completely out; although we did manage to pass a few words of conversation during the course of the day. This chit-chat was mainly about films, boyfriends and gossip in general. We even had the occasional singsong – mostly on paydays – until we were told to shut up.

By this time the war had taken on a more serious note. The Battle of Britain had already been fought and we'd been unaware of the seriousness of it. Ration books had been issued and we were finding it difficult to buy make-up and things like polish and imported fruit.

Notices appeared in the press and on hoardings encouraging young people to join up – women as well. People were also needed to help on the land and women were volunteering to join the so-called 'Land Army' to help the farmers grow as much food and cattle as possible. This rather appealed to me. I'd always loved the countryside. I thought about it quite a lot.

I was never one to read much in the newspaper but I kept my eyes open for the advertisements of the Land Army. None of the entry forms seemed to have a minimum age limit so I naturally assumed one could join anytime after leaving school. I made up my mind and decided to join. I mentioned this to my parents and was surprised at their down-cry. They didn't like the idea of me living away from home and went on to mention damp beds and awful food and that I was too young anyway. The more they said against it, the more I wanted to join. Eventually, I filled in an application form from the press and sent it off. I didn't tell my parents.

Each day I waited for a reply. All my thoughts were centred on the work I would do on a farm and what it would be like to live away from home. I'd never lived away from home before.

About two weeks later a postcard arrived for me in

answer to my application. It was a typed card saying simply that I was too young to go into the Land Army but I could try again when I was older. This threw me and I was shattered. I had no idea I would be turned down, least of all because I was too young. I had really geared myself to leaving home and standing on my own two feet and suddenly everything had fallen flat. All these dreams I had of working on a farm, and the fact that I would be independent – all gone. That and the ridicule of my parents took me days to recover. In the end I lost all interest in the Land Army and consoled myself with the thought that I would join one of the services. I would have to wait until I was 17 and a half, but that is what I decided to do.

The weeks went by and I looked more closely at the girls in uniform. I spoke to the girls at work about joining up, and one or two said, they would join with me when the time came, that is if the firm we worked for would release us. I asked them what they meant by "if the firm would release us". It was then that I learned I was in a reserved occupation. This meant that the work I was doing was of national importance and skilled civilian labour was as vital to the war effort as the men in the front line. This also applied to many other jobs, such as munitions and foundries. I couldn't leave my job if I wanted to, not without release from the firm, and I was told they released only in very special circumstances.

I accepted this information without question. I had no idea that I was in a reserved occupation and that to leave would not be easy. This was food for thought. I would have to think of some way of getting my release if I were to join one of the services. It was bad enough having to wait a year to join up without any complications to contend with.

A few days later I was in the loo for a break — there were no tea breaks in those days — and I heard someone saying she'd received a letter from her young brother in the Forces. She went on to say how he had lied about his age so that he could get into the R.A.F. My ears pricked up, but I could glean no more from that conversation and I couldn't ask because I shouldn't have been listening in the first place! My imagination began to work overtime. This was really something. The thought of lying about my age had never occurred to me. For days I could think of nothing else.

Each night I went to bed early and, in the quiet of my room, tried to dream up a scheme that would enable me to join up without having to wait a year. The only snag I could see was giving my notice in at the factory. Suppose they wouldn't release me. I had to think of something where I could get away with no questions asked, bearing in mind that I was only 16 and a half.

It was about this time that mass evacuation was taking place all over the country. School children in areas where there was heavy bombing were being sent to live in the more quiet, less industrial zones. Evacuation was taking place in Ipswich and two of my sisters were going to be sent to Northampton with others from their school. My mother also had the chance to go but insisted on staying at home to look after my father and the younger children.

This, I thought, could be the answer to my problem. I would tell the firm that I was being evacuated with the rest of my family. There would be nothing they could do about that. Having made up my mind completely I set out to join the Women's Auxiliary Air Force. I filled in an application form from the newspaper and put my age as 18 next birthday and sent it off. I waited anxiously for a reply hoping that there would be no slip-ups this time. I said nothing to my parents.

The answer duly arrived and with it the information that I was to attend a medical examination in London. I was over the moon with excitement. My parents had very little to say but I hardly noticed. My mind was filled with all kinds of thoughts. Would I pass the medical and could I get away with my age? How long would it be before I actually left home and what would it be like serving my country in uniform? I wondered what sort of job I would do and if I would be homesick. I'd never been out of Ipswich before, apart from the occasional trip to the seaside. I must be prepared for homesickness I told myself.

The trip to London for my medical was quite an experience for me. I had to call in at the local recruitment office to pick up my railway warrant. There I was given directions as to where to go and how to get there. I remember it was High Holborn. I had to make my way on my own and, although I was excited, I was not a bit worried about the prospect. The only thing that did bother me was that somehow someone would find out my age. I was supposed to have taken my birth certificate with me, but conveniently forgot it! I told them it had been mislaid. Lies and more lies! I was beginning to wonder how many more I would have to tell. I remembered something my grandmother was always saying, "Be sure your sins will find you out."

I passed my medical OK – that was a relief. I then had to go for an interview with a W.A.A.F. Officer. She asked me all sorts of questions about my work and school and asked which trade I would like to take up in the service. I told her I would like to be a driver. My father had been a driver since he was 16 and had driven all sorts of vehicles from fruit lorries to buses. I had thought about this a great deal and had imagined myself driving around the countryside with dispatches or even taking officers to conferences. The officer looked at me steadily and told me about the responsibility of a driving job. She mentioned driving through bombing raids and getting casualties to hospital. She thought I was rather young for that kind of job. I didn't argue. The mere mention of the word "young" and my defences were up. I didn't want to rock the boat now that I had got this far. She suggested I followed my own trade of tailoring and this I agreed to do.

From there I was guided to another room where there were many more recruits like myself. We had the 'Oath of Allegiance' explained to us and we were consequently sworn in.

Having completed all that, I was then informed that I was a member of H.M. Forces and I would be sent for in due course, probably in a few weeks' time, and I would be given ten days before reporting for duty.

It was all over, no hitches. I was in. I really couldn't believe it. I travelled home with my head in the clouds. All I had to do now was wait. I hoped it wouldn't be long.

Chapter 2

Into Uniform

JUNE 21st – my 17th birthday – and still no word. I wondered about the delay as the weeks dragged themselves around. I was afraid that the war might be over before I could do 'my bit'. Then on the 8th July I received the orders calling me to active service. A railway warrant was enclosed and details of what to take with me. I was very excited but there was no one to share my enthusiasm.

With my two sisters in Northampton, there were only my parents who were non-committal. They didn't discourage me, nor did they encourage me. I think they had their own particular worries at the time. Bombing was getting more frequent and heavier and almost every item of food was rationed in one form or another. They probably had enough to cope with without me adding to their troubles. Some of the girls at work were pleased for me and some just refused to believe me. I don't know why.

I gave in my notice on the pretext of evacuation just as I had planned and I managed to get my cards with no problem at all (I have wondered since, if there would have been any bother anyway, but I couldn't afford to take the chance). I worked out one week's notice and said goodbye to my workmates.

The next couple of days were very sunny and warm. All

of my friends were at work so I spent these days on my own, swimming, cycling, and sunbathing. I tried hard to impress on my memory places familiar to me, which I could recall should I get homesick.

I had to report to Innsworth near Gloucester on 18th July 1941 at 10am. To be able to report at the hours stated, I would have to travel the day before. That meant I would have to find somewhere in Gloucester to stay for the night. My parents agreed so I decided to do just that. I don't suppose the authorities would have minded if I had reported at six in the evening, but I wanted to start off on the right foot.

It was a hot sunny day for travelling and, to add to my discomfort, the stiff pile on the carriage seats poked through my thin cotton dress to aggravate the sunburn on my back. It was a long journey. I had to change trains in London. I crossed to Paddington and boarded the train to Gloucester. I hadn't spoken to a soul all day and was beginning to tire of my own company. Sitting opposite me was a man, much older than myself, in khaki uniform. He passed a few polite words at first and later started to chat freely. He asked me where I was going and when I told him he curled up laughing. I felt a bit embarrassed, as I didn't understand his humour at all. He must have realised how I felt as he lowered his voice and started to speak quietly. "I suppose you know what you are letting yourself in for," he said. "In the first place, the porridge you get will be so thick you'll need a knife and fork to eat it and don't eat the stew." He went on, "They make that from the stray dogs and cats that roam around the camp." I giggled, disbelieving every word. The more I laughed the more ridiculous he became. In no time at all we were at Gloucester. He wished me well and I left him on the train. I made my way into the city with my sides still aching from the recent laughter.

By now it was early evening and I wanted to find myself somewhere to sleep as soon as possible. I daren't think what I'd do if I couldn't find a place. I hadn't eaten since breakfast and I was hungry. I had been so excited when I started out that morning that I hadn't given food a thought. I didn't much like the idea of eating on my own so I hoped I could get something to eat at my digs when I found them. I had no ration card to offer, only my ration book which I had to hand in at the camp. Needless to say the rations had already been used for the current week. I lived in the hope that everything would be all right.

Finding bed and breakfast was not as bad as I had anticipated. I found my way to the road that led to Innsworth and in the window of several of the houses was a 'Bed & Breakfast' sign. I picked one at random and knocked on the door. I must admit, I was a little apprehensive at the prospect of sleeping in an unknown place but I needn't have worried. My landlady made me very welcome and she cut me some sandwiches and promised to call me early the next day. I think I must have fallen asleep as soon as my head touched the pillow. I slept like a log and was awakened the next morning with a hot cup of tea. It took me a couple of seconds to figure out where I was. I had had a most comfortable night and enjoyed my breakfast.

I took a bus to the W.A.A.F. Reception Centre at Innsworth and reported to the guardroom as ordered. There were others in the same position as myself and I was relieved to find that I was no longer alone.

After we had all been checked in we were given a knife, fork and spoon and a huge white mug. We had to sign for them and we were warned not to let them out of our sight, as they were the only means of eating our meals. We were to wash them up after use and carry them always while on the station. I didn't relish walking across the camp with a mug in my hand but, as I had nowhere to put it, I had to and so did the others. I noticed later that this was common practice.

We were shown to our billet, which was a long wooden hut. Inside were a number of single iron beds with a steel locker at the side of each one. This was where we were to sleep for the next two weeks while we were doing our square bashing. At one end of the hut was a small room, which was occupied by the N.C.O.* in charge of the billet. She was there to answer any of our queries and to enforce order.

I barely had time to unpack my things before we were whisked away to the cookhouse for a meal. The dining hall was very big, filled with long tables with forms each side on which to sit. Some of the tables were reserved for the N.C.O.s and the rest were used by the Sprogs (new recruits) and other ranks. The serving hatch was as big as an average size bar with the main course served at one end and the sweet at the other. In front of the servery was a trestle table holding two urns of tea – one sweet and one not. Also on the table was a large pan of warm water, which was for washing our knife, fork and spoon after eating. It was quite early for lunch and we had all of the hall to ourselves so we

* N.C.O. – Non-commissioned officers = Corporal, Sergeant, or Flight Sergeant.

had our meal and washed our irons in the clean warm water. I was to find out afterwards that the clean water we used was still there for the latecomer. By then it looked more like a bowl of soup!

We were issued with sheets and pillow cover and given instructions of laundry procedure and bed making. Each morning all bed linen and blankets had to be folded and stacked in a neat pile at the head of the bed.

Then came the F.F.I. This was a 'free from infection' examination that was carried out on all persons posted to or going from an R.A.F. Station. It was a precaution against infection, disease and lice. Not only did posted persons have the F.F.I. but all personnel were subject to it once a month, no matter who or where they were. These examinations took place in the M.I. (medical inspection) room and were carried out by the Medical Officer and staff. Checks were made on weight, height, ears, nose and throat. Fingers and toes were looked at and heart and lungs were sounded. The whole thing didn't take more than two minutes. Everyone had to strip to the waist and file in one by one. There was no room for modesty and, although at first, I was most embarrassed I eventually got used to it.

I have no idea how many recruits passed through this W.A.A.F. reception centre each week, but the figure must have run into hundreds. The camp itself was quite a big place and discipline was as strict as possible for the host of newcomers.

The ablutions were communal with long rows of toilets, hand basins, shower units and baths. There was hot water but this was soon run off with the vast numbers using taps at the same time. All baths and sinks were expected to be left clean by the people who used them and everyone was warned about sneak thieves and advised not to leave rings and watches in such places.

At the end of my first day I felt I had been there for a week. So much had been crammed into those first few hours. From what I could see there were two entirely different ways of living – the civilian life and the service life – I could find no common bond between them except, maybe, eating and sleeping. Such was my impression at the time.

I wrote to my parents in the evening to let them know I had arrived OK and to tell them about my journey. Strangely enough I didn't feel homesick. I thought I might have done by now, but I was lapping up every single minute. With so much to learn and so many people to talk to from so many different places, I suppose I was too preoccupied to think much about anything else.

The whole two weeks that followed were jam-packed with lectures, gas drills and fire drills. There was so much to do in so little time. We learned about R.A.F. procedure. There was a right way to go about everything and being well informed was the only key to survival.

We had lectures on hygiene. As you can imagine, this was very high on the list of importance with all of us living so closely in a confined area. It was here we were told about venereal diseases and I was utterly amazed to learn how common they are. I thought perhaps V.D. was something that came with senility. Sanitary towels were provided at the guardroom when required. These had to be signed for and disposed of in the proper manner – usually a covered bucket in the ablutions. They were then taken to the incinerator and burned by whoever was on ablution duty.

Uniforms had to be kept clean, pressed and worn cor-
rectly with all the buttons fastened and no bulging pockets.
Hair must be worn neat and tidy one inch above the collar.
My hair was very long and I found it quite a problem. If I
piled my hair on top of my head I couldn't get my hat on
and, if I curled it tight all night then by midday it was
hanging around my shoulders. I had to do something about
it and the only thing I could think of was to cut it off. I
borrowed some nail scissors from one of the girls and set
about cutting my own hair. I thought that by measuring
each clump of hair with my fingers and then snipping it off it
must finish level all the way round. That was my theory so
that's what I did – over and over again – then some bright
spark piped up and said there was a hairdresser on the camp.
It was too late to go to her then, as I would have had no hair
left! My hair was definitely above my collar and that had
been the object of the exercise. I dread to think what I must
have looked like and I didn't try to do that again.

Pilfering was a hazard that could only be controlled by
keeping everything under lock and key. Everyone was
warned against lending money or anything else of value.
"Trust no one," was the motto "not even your best
friend."

The transformation of persons that occurred after drawing
our kit from stores was almost unbelievable. Girls who
looked positively stunning in their civilian clothes in some
cases changed to a dull blob of grey. Others who were not so
fashion conscious came out looking like a million dollars,
and some just looked a complete mess. I think it was really a
question of adjustment. After a couple of days in uniform
everyone seemed to find a similar level of smartness.

The issue of undies had to be seen to be believed. The bras were made of strong pink cotton material and shaped to fit the flattest chest. If the chest wasn't flat to start with, it was after putting on a service bra. Pure wool vests with high round necks – today we would probably have used them as pullovers. The bloomers of navy interlock fitted like the bottom half of a 1920's swimsuit. Not much fear of catching cold wearing that lot, in fact there wasn't much fear of anything! Civilian clothing was completely banned but later on I do think most girls wore their own frilly knicks when they could get them.

Knotting neckties was a problem that had to be overcome. Not one of the girls I was billeted with had ever worn a tie before, and collar studs were a complete mystery. After a while we called the corporal in to show us the best way to tackle the job. Once the tie was knotted it was common practice to leave it that way. To take it off we simply loosened it and slipped it over our heads. It was then ready to slip on again when needed.

Marching and counter marching, about turning and changing step was all learned by numbers. The drill sergeant had a voice that must have shaken the foundations of Gloucester Cathedral! Respirators and tin helmets had to be carried at all times, slung over the right shoulder when on parade and hanging loosely on the left when walking out. This left the right arm free to salute.

Respirator cases were frequently used as handbags by the W.A.A.F. Some of the girls removed the respirator completely to make more room for their personal things. Heaven knows how they would have got on if there had been a gas raid. At least they would not have died with a shiny nose! We learned how to deal with incendiary bombs, bomb blast and how to treat someone in shock. Care of the individual was most important. A severe case of sunburn was considered a crime. Loss of working hours resulting from this kind of negligence was classed as sabotage. I found this out when I attended my F.F.I. and the medical officer saw the blisters on my back!

Our term of initial training was nearly over although there were still a few lectures to attend. These were mostly to inform us of the fundamental laws of the service. Daily Routine Orders were explained to us as being exactly what they were called. These orders were posted daily on the station notice board, which was always situated outside the guardroom of any camp. They were directed specifically to all personnel or to the individual as the case maybe, and were to be read daily. In no circumstances were they to be ignored or forgotten. Failure to read or abide by them could lead to a charge.

A charge is an accusation or summons of a sort that has to be answered and is usually brought about by defaulting in some way. This was a way of curbing disobedience of the service rules. Punishment could be almost any sort of restriction such as being confined to camp for a given period or maybe extra work after normal working hours. To be placed on a charge for a misdemeanour was not uncommon, but something everyone tried to avoid. It was embarrassing and degrading.

At the end of our training we had 'Passing Out Parade' to mark the occasion. It seemed incredible that only two weeks before this we were all civilians. Now we were all ready to move on and train for whatever job we had joined up to do.

All we had to do now was wait for a posting. No one knew when it would come or where it would be.

During the next couple of days while I was waiting for my posting I was put to work in the administration block. I had no idea of what I was supposed to be doing and I don't think anyone else did either. It was a stopgap I suppose, I couldn't just sit around doing nothing. I fetched and carried odd pieces of paper from one office to another. Everyone seemed to be working hard except me. It wasn't very pleasant. There were so many officers around and I had to keep saluting. It was not until I had knocked a tray of papers flying while trying to salute in a confined area with my left

This is a photo of me taken in 1943 – now on exhibition at Flixton Air Museum.

31

hand, that someone told me there was no need, as I wasn't wearing a hat! I attended the next Postings Parade almost praying!

I was quite surprised to see how our numbers had dwindled as already more than half of our group had gone. We all waited anxiously as the list of names was read out wondering if we were the next to go and if so, where.

At last my name was called but I had to wait for about a couple of dozen more names before I knew where I was going. The agony of that wait was almost unbearable. The station must be a big one, I thought, if all these people were being posted there. The last name was finally called and then it was announced that we were all posted to 32 M.U. St Athan, Glamorgan, South Wales. This was the largest camp in the country.

Chapter 3

Postings and Parachutes

ST Athan, R.A.F. Station was situated a couple of miles east of the village of Llantwit Major on the south coast of Glamorganshire. The station itself was divided into two halves, 32 M.U. (Maintenance Unit) was on one side and what was called the 'hutted camp' on the other and in between them was the airfield. They were joined only by the perimeter around the airstrip. The only other way of getting from one to the other was to use the public road leading from Llantwit Major to St Athan village going out of the main gate of one and along the road to the main gate of the other. It was indeed a big station. I was told it was one of the largest in the world, second only to Singapore. Personnel numbered nearly 4,000 then and a quarter of them were WAAF.

The hutted camp was exactly what the name implied. Among other things there was a school for flight mechanics. There was a large indoor swimming pool, hard and grass tennis courts, playing fields and a hangar that had been converted into a huge cinema with a change of programme every two days and again on Sundays.

The maintenance unit seemed small in comparison but, nevertheless, quite a big unit. Here repairs and modifications were carried out on all sorts of equipment and the work was brought in from bases all over the country. The workshops, where most of the personnel worked, were many and varied. Instruments, engines, wireless, armoury and parachutes to name but a few.

Each side of the camp had its own administration and one was not to be confused with the other. Friendly rivalry existed between the two sides.

Football, cricket, hockey and netball were but a few of the sports organised between, not only the hutted camp and the M.U. but nearby camps and villages.

There was plenty to do in the evenings such as camp concerts, dances and talent competitions. There were evening classes for such pastimes as chess, languages, playing the bagpipes, etc. Of course, if we wanted to get away from the atmosphere of the R.A.F. then outside entertainment was the answer. Barry was just eight miles away by train and there was Cardiff and Bridgend although, most of the time, the great majority only went to these places at weekends when there was more time to travel.

All W.A.A.F. personnel on 32 M.U. was billeted in married quarters. These houses had as many beds in each room as was possible and a chair or cabinet if you were lucky. Uniform and personal belongings had to be kept in a case or kit bag, which was kept under the bed. Thursday night was 'domestic night'. Everyone was confined to camp on that night each week for the sole purpose of cleaning the billets. Each bed space was cleaned daily by the occupier but Thursday was the day for the bigger household chores. Passes on that day were issued only with special permission.

Although accommodation was cramped there was a certain amount of privacy, which didn't exist at Innsworth.

One could at least write a letter without the interruptions and the gossip of a dozen other girls. No door was ever locked, not even at night. The Orderly Officer had access at all time, either to inspect during the day or to make sure lights were out. We were never sure if or when she would decide to visit.

The whole of the W.A.A.F. living quarters were out of bounds to all males and this was strictly adhered to. The same applied to females in men's quarters. The R.A.F. lived in three-storey blocks of dormitories on the other side of the unit. I shared a room with two other girls on the ground floor of my billet − it was probably the sitting room of the house. There was no furniture at all so each of us had to make do with our cases and kit bags. At night, when I undressed for bed, I would fold my uniform neatly and lie it on the floor at the side of my bed. This prevented it from becoming creased in my kit bag and it was ready to jump into the next morning.

One night we were awakened by someone fumbling with the handle of the door to our room. It opened and a very bright torch beam shone round on each of us in turn. We were all startled. It was the Orderly Officer and Sergeant. The torch beam settled on my clothes on the floor.

"Whose uniform is this?" said the stern voice. I was half asleep but admitted to ownership. "Why is it on the floor?" The light in the room was switched on and I could then see both of them. The officer went on, "Why can't you fold it properly and put it on the bottom of your bed?"

I replied, "Because if I did I'd probably kick it off in the night and it would end up crumpled on the floor anyway."

Without further question I was charged with "wilful

neglect of the King's uniform". I'm not sure of the exact words but they meant the same, and I was told to report the following morning. This I did, feeling rather unsure of myself and very nervous. The sergeant told me to remove my hat and to stand between two other waafs. I didn't know who they were.

Then she surprised me by shouting "Attention". We all three straightened up. "Left turn" and "Forward march, Left wheel" – we were in front of the Officers' desk! "Halt" and "Left turn." I was truly surprised and wondered what was coming next. I wouldn't have been surprised to see a firing squad!

After the charge was read out to me I was asked if I had anything to say. I repeated what I had said the night before. It made no difference. I was sentenced to seven days extra duties. We were marched outside and dismissed. My hat was returned to me and the sergeant explained how and when to report. I was then sent back to the workshop.

The charge was over but there was worse to come. Not only was I confined to camp for seven days, but I had to report to the guardroom every hour, on the hour, when I was not on duty or doing fatigues. Each time I reported I was inspected. I had to make sure that I was properly dressed, my cap, badge, buttons were sparkling, shoes shining and my hair tidy above my collar. Any default here and I would have been put on another charge. Not only that, but I had to report to the cookhouse sergeant after my days work and it was up to her to give me extra duties.

I had never been behind the servery in the dining hall, so had no idea of what to expect and I wouldn't have expected what I saw, even if I had been told! I was given the job of washing up the big pans that had been used to cook the meals of the day. I could hardly handle them, they were so heavy and awkward and the food was baked on so hard it was almost impossible to get off. With all the ovens in use cooking something or other, the place was very hot, and cockroaches were abundant everywhere. There were duck-boards to stand on by the deep sinks and these were almost floating in water that was lying everywhere. Outside were bins of swill from the day's leftovers and the smell was putrid. This attracted swarms of bluebottles and flies. I was up to my elbows in warm greasy water that seemed to get dirtier at the sight of the containers I was trying to clean. I was never more glad when that night was over. I dreaded the next six nights that followed, I thought the week would never end. Those seven days taught me a lesson that I wasn't to forget for a long while.

Some months later I had my hat stolen from the cloak-room in the dining hall. I didn't dare report it for fear of being charged with negligence so, without hesitation, I pinched someone else's. I was learning!

Why I was posted to St Athan I shall never know. When I was asked where I would like to be posted, I had asked for the East Coast, although I didn't really mind where I went. The point was that when I got to St Athan there were no vacancies for tailors so I had to be given another job. The nearest job to tailoring that they could find was parachute repairing! I had no choice and it was useless to argue now. I didn't know one end of a parachute from another, nor did any of the other girls who were going to do the same work, but there was no cause for alarm. We'd all be taught every-thing we needed to know in due course – at least that's what

I thought. All the girls working in the parachute repair shop were billeted together or nearby and, so it was for the other working sections. There were several of us girls from Innsworth, as well as a couple from Bridgenorth, the other W.A.A.F. reception centre. We sprogs all reported to the workshop at the same time so we all started off together.

The work we were to do was explained to us very thoroughly from start to finish, but that was all. We had no tuition. We watched others working and learned a little there. It seemed to be a question of making ourselves look busy and no one seemed to mind what we did as long as we were occupied. Sewing machines were limited and constantly being used for repairs by those who had already learned the job. If a machine became idle for a while then we were allowed to practice. Some of the girls starting had never used a sewing machine before so I would forego my turn at a machine to allow one of them to have a go.

The 'chutes came in from all parts of the country. They were usually damaged in some way and had to be patched. Sometimes a whole panel would have to be replaced which meant a great deal of unpicking and this had to be done with great care so as not to damage any other panel of the 'chute. I spent a lot of my time doing this and so did the others. Sometimes there would be several of us working on one 'chute.

Over the other side of the workshop were some very long polished tables. These were used by the men for packing 'chutes. I had watched them working while I was unpicking and failed to see how they could get such a large volume of material into such a small compact bundle. I had to find out so, one day when there was nothing much for me to do, I ventured over to one of the fellows and watched him at work. His name was Les and he made the job look so simple and he was very informative. After I had watched him pack a couple of 'chutes he asked me if I'd like to have a try. I was delighted. He had to get permission first, but that was OK, so I went ahead with Les instructing me.

I managed to get the right posture with half my bottom on the table. Then I had to open and fold each panel separately, which meant me moving my arms up in such a fashion that I could hardly keep my balance. I carried on but the silk seemed to have a mind of its own and was not in agreement with mine! Next the riggings. These were packed with a large hook and finally – the ripcord. I was finished but could hardly believe the untidiness of the bundle I had created. It was one big sloppy mess!

Les smiled and, with great patience, undid it all and let me try again. From then on I spent most of my time on the packing table. Before very long I was able to pack a 'chute reasonably well. Most of the 'chutes, having been repaired in our workshop, were packed for dispatch only. That meant they would be repacked for service use when they reached their destination. We rarely packed for service use, but, of course, there was always the exception to the rule.

There was one occasion when I packed a 'chute for service – or at least that's what I was led to believe. It was brought into the workshop by a crew member who wanted to see it packed. Apparently all aircrew were given this option although many of them chose to ignore it. I was packing a 'chute for dispatch at the time and he waited while watching me. Then he asked me to do this job for him. I explained that I was only learning and had no authority to

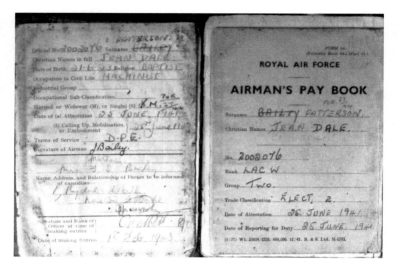

This Pay Book is on exhibition at Flixton Airport Museum — it contains all records of medicals, trade boards and pay, etc.

pack for service so referred him to Les. He said, he didn't want Les. He was perfectly willing to take his chance with me! I did the job while Les supervised and took full responsibility. He thanked me and went on his way. I don't know who he was or if he ever had to use his 'chute. I only know I never saw him again.

By now I was getting used to life in the service. My fears of homesickness had long since passed and I considered myself very fortunate. I wrote home regularly and looked forward to my first leave. I had already spent a 48-hour pass in Cardiff Y.W.C.A. on my own and I didn't enjoy it much. I spent most of my time looking at shops and going to the cinema. I really didn't know quite what to do with myself. There hadn't been enough time for me to get to Ipswich and back, not if I wanted any time at home. I wasn't sorry when that pass was over.

I was also getting to know the girls I worked with and my room-mates. Some of them spoke so broadly in their own local dialects that I found it difficult to understand what they were saying. I expect some of them had a similar problem listening to me and my Suffolk accent, but gradually I was able to understand the different dialects and became good at it later. I would know which part of the country they were from just by listening to them. Having mastered the art of listening then conversation became much easier and life more interesting.

Chapter 4

Remustering

THE little village of Llantwit Major was a fair walk from camp but it made for a very pleasant stroll when the evenings were warm. I think there were nearly as many pubs as there were private dwellings. The small cinema had a change of programme twice a week so we had a good selection of films to see. The trouble was I had already seen most films that were shown here and on camp, but I would occasionally go to see one through again. There was a big Y.M.C.A. in the village where tea and sandwiches were always available. There were also a couple of fish and chip shops, which proved to be very popular although there was very seldom any fish to be had. About half a mile further on was the Bristol Channel – too many boulders for safe swimming but very cool to the feet!

The village was always bubbling over with R.A.F. bods* in the evenings – it was about the only place to go to get any refreshments other than the N.A.A.F.I. There was a bus service to the camp should anyone be too tired to walk the journey back, or was too late. We had to be in by 10.15pm unless we had a late pass, which expired at midnight. Goings and comings of all personnel was checked at the guardroom.

* Bods = R.A.F. personnel.

We had to report on the way out of camp and again on the way in, showing our passes as we did so.

The day had been fine and the evening promised to be cool and ideal for a ramble. Gwen, who also worked in the parachute section and shared the same billet, and I decided to take a walk to the village and perhaps go on to the sea. There were the usual crowds out for their evening relaxation so we decided to discover what was beyond the road. There was a small beaten track that led us into some woods and very pleasant it was too. A small stream made the place even prettier and the wild flowers grew without hindrance. It was hard to realise we were still in the vicinity of camp. We rambled on and before long the path led out to the sea. It was a beautiful evening and after a while we headed back to camp.

We had plenty of time so we agreed to stop and get some chips in the village fish shop, and eat them as we walked home. As usual there was quite a queue and while we were waiting we stood talking to three chaps who had joined the queue after us. The fish shop was a very clean, neat place and very small. In the shop window was a big brass curtain rail that held up a short green curtain, about five feet off the ground. The brass rail shone with regular cleaning and the curtain looked new or else it was well laundered. For the sake of something to talk about I remarked on how smart the curtain rail looked. One of the fellows laughed and said, "How would you like it in your billet?"

I answered saying, "It would look much better than the royal-blue black-out curtains we have at the moment." Gwen was already being served, so I hastened to get my money ready. We picked up our chips and walked out.

We hadn't gone far and there was hooting and whistling from behind us. It was the boys from the fish shop who were yelling for us to wait, which we did, and we all walked back to camp together eating our chips. It was then that they told us they were from the hutted camp and were on the flight mechanics course. Apparently they had just come out of the cinema when they met us in the queue. We chatted about this and that and, in no time at all we were almost at the gates of 32 M.U. The boys of course had to walk further. Suddenly one of them thrust this great bundle of something at me and then the three of them ran off. It was the curtain from the fish shop! Gwen and I just stared at each other neither knowing quite what to do. We stopped at the side of the road trying hard to conceal it from others walking back to camp. What were we to do? We had to hide it somehow before we got back to the main gate. Gwen suggested we folded the curtain as best we could and tuck it in our tunic. Once we got past the main gate we could take it to our billet, hide it and then book in at the guardroom. I agreed. When we went to fold it we found the curtain was in two pieces so Gwen had one and I had the other. We walked through the gate looking like two very busty waafs. Our hearts were in our mouths and we couldn't get to the billet fast enough. We hid the curtains in between our bed covers and went to book in.

How on earth were we going to get rid of it? To try to get it back to the fish shop was only asking for trouble. The fish shop was sure to miss it soon and may even get in touch with the camp police. If they were to do that then I would be up the creek. Each billet would be searched until it was found. I had to get rid of it quickly. The only thing I could think of was to parcel it up and send it off to my mother. I could slip a note in with it telling her not to mention it in her letters. Letters and parcels were sometimes censored going out of camp but I'd have to take a chance on that.

I suggested this idea to Gwen and she could think of nothing better. Next day the parcel was posted and I didn't rest easy for a couple of days after that. Nothing more was heard of the green curtain but my mother was delighted! I never did explain to her how I had received it. I didn't go out of the camp for some time after that. I was half afraid I'd meet up with those boys again and that was the last thing I wanted to happen. They had caused me enough worry as it was.

Nellie, my room-mate was always asking me to go with her to the dance, which was held regularly in the gym or N.A.A.F.I. I'd never been inside a dance hall in my life so I always declined. There was to be a big dance on the following Saturday and she asked me again. I told her it was pointless as I just hadn't a clue how to dance. Without hesitation she said she would teach me. This was a chance I couldn't miss so I accepted gracefully.

That week we nearly wore out the floor in the N.A.A.F.I. trying to dance to numbers, one, two, three, one, two, three, as we had no music. Nellie was quite pleased with my progress and I was surprised to find it was so easy, never guessing for one moment that I had only learned one part of the many different dances. It was all ballroom dancing then and only the occasional pair would jitterbug.

I began to look forward to the dance in the gym, perhaps things would be OK, after all. I got myself dressed up in my best blue and off we went. Lots of the other girls were there too and sat chatting and listening to the music. It was not long before someone asked me to dance. It was a waltz and I enjoyed it – dancing to music was great. I came out of that all right. This was fun I thought and settled down to enjoy the evening. My enjoyment soon came to an end, however, when the M.C. decided to make an announcement. After calling for silence he told us how sorry he was to announce that the lead saxophone player had been reported missing and presumed lost. He was an air gunner and had not returned from a recent raid on Germany. The M.C. called for a one minute silence to pay our respects. The girls were stunned, as they knew the chap well by sight. He had always played with that particular band at the camp dances. I didn't know him but that didn't alter the fact that I couldn't carry on dancing after that. I left and so did several more.

It was some time before I went dancing again and by that time Nellie had taught me most of the other dances as well. I must admit that I had some very enjoyable evenings on the dance floor and will always be grateful to Nellie for her tolerance and patience in teaching me.

Sunday on camp was a lazy day. Breakfast was always a bit later than usual. Lots of girls didn't bother with breakfast but would lie in bed late and get up for dinner at midday. For tea we always had cheese and beetroot. This was a recognised feature on Sundays.

I'd been for a stroll with the girls down to the sea and came back with quite an edge to my appetite. I had a rather large helping of beetroot and enjoyed it. Next morning I went to the toilet and my urine was pink! I was puzzled and a little bit worried. I told Nellie who was a bit disturbed and advised me to go sick. I was really worried when she said that. I didn't go to breakfast, as I just couldn't have eaten anything. I wasn't ill, just concerned about my well-being. I reported sick. I hardly knew what to say to the M.O. as it was so embarrassing, but I finally manage to blurt it out. She grinned and asked me if I had eaten any beetroot recently! I was so relieved, as I had no idea that beetroot could have that effect on anyone. I came out of the M.I. room[*] walking on air. I wished then that I had gone to breakfast!

Each morning around 10 o'clock we had a break for 10 minutes. It was usually triggered by the arrival of the N.A.A.F.I. wagon. We would queue with our service mugs for tea and wads (cakes). The cakes were a kind of rock bun with hardly any sweetness in them owing to sugar rationing. Nevertheless, they could taste very sweet if someone was hungry. The wagon came in the afternoon too, but seldom had any wads. Anyone who wanted to eat during the afternoon was well advised to buy in the morning. I breakfasted on N.A.A.F.I. wads.

After dinner I read D.R.O.s[†] and found my name amongst those for inoculation parade at 2pm. This just wasn't my day. I had my jab and went back to work. I did nothing with the advice given me by everyone on ways to ease the discomfort of inoculation, and just carried on packing 'chutes. At 3 o'clock we had our afternoon break and some of the girls were already complaining of stiffness in their arms. I didn't feel any stiffness in mine and I think it was because I had been using it for so much work. The girls consoled themselves with a cigarette but I didn't smoke.

[*] M.I. = Medical Inspection room.
[†] D.R.O. = Daily Routine Orders.

Jenny insisted that I had one. "With the day you have had it will do you good and ease the tension," she said. Reluctantly I took one and lit it. I didn't like the taste much. "Ah, that's because you are not inhaling," said Jenny. She showed me what she meant. I took a large puff and thought my lungs would burst. I coughed and spluttered much to the amusement of the other girls. I had another go – not such a big one this time. "That's better," said my smoking friend. I finished the cigarette inhaling only a couple of times more.

Break was over and we went into work but I was beginning to feel shaky. It wasn't long before I began to feel sick. I felt really bad and looked it by all accounts. If only I could have vomited I think I would have felt easier. It was an hour or so before I began to feel a bit better. I blamed the cigarette, but Jenny blamed the inoculation. I wasn't sure. The other girls hadn't felt ill like me.

I was glad when work was over and I was able to get back to my billet and have a lie down. Jenny came in to see me and offered me a cigarette. I wanted to ram it down her throat! Very quietly she told me that I'd feel much better if I just had a puff at one. She was so convincing that I finally took one. It didn't make me feel ill but I was still shaky. Afterwards I began to feel better. Next day I had another and soon I was smoking regularly.

With leave coming up I was wondering what my parents would say when they saw me smoking. They both liked a cigarette but, somehow, I felt it would not meet with their approval. I was looking forward to my holiday and didn't want anything to spoil it. I had two choices – I could tell them or I could keep it from them. In the end I decided to write and tell them. I had a letter in return saying how much they were looking forward to seeing me. Smoking wasn't mentioned. I was glad of that and didn't worry about it anymore.

Leave time came round and I travelled home for the first time in uniform. It was October 1941. When I arrived my sister Kit was waiting for me at the station. She was just 15 months younger than me, and seemed to have grown up quite a bit since I last saw her. All the family were pleased to see me and Dad looked me over with a critical eye. There was so much to say and plenty to talk about but, for some reason, I was quite speechless. I eventually found my tongue but just couldn't tell them a lot about my work or environment. Somehow, I felt they would never understand.

In no time at all I was in civilian clothes. They felt so light and flimsy after the uniform and I felt quite feminine again. It was good to be at home looking at the familiar sights and faces. Kit took a couple of days off work to keep me company. She was working at the local silk factory making ladies underwear. We had a look around town and visited relatives. I listened to gossip and heard the latest news on the bombing and air raids. I had almost forgotten the sound of the 'Alert'. We didn't have raids at St Athan but we could hear the gunfire when Cardiff or Bristol had a raid.

The week slipped by so quickly and once again I was on the train going back to camp. I had enjoyed my leave and was already starting to look forward to the next. I didn't mind going back to camp and wondered if anything exciting had happened on the unit while I had been away.

A few days after my return the Warrant Officer in charge of the Parachute Section called a dozen of us into his office. He explained to us that the trade of the parachute repairer

Update of my 1250. (Identity Card)

had now been closed and he didn't know if or when there would be any more vacancies. All he could offer us was a job in either the electrical or the armoury workshop. There were six vacancies in each, and we had a day to decide between ourselves who was going where.

None of us fancied the work we had been offered but, the choice had to be made. I decided I would take the electrical work – at least it might be helpful in civvy street. Having made our decisions, arrangements were made for our remuster. This took no time at all and with the new job came a new billet. We had to remove ourselves from the girls in Parachute Sections and go to live with the other girls in armoury and electrical workshops.

Each job in the service was graded according to skill and

ability required. These grades were numbered one to five. No waaf was considered capable of Grade I. There was an odd occasion when a waaf might be considered for Grade II but the majority were put into jobs that came within the Grades III to V. Each grade had its own scale of pay with Grade V being the lowest. With no trade in view and very little service behind me my pay was at rock bottom, and I was completely unaware of anything I could do to help myself. I didn't brood over this turn of events, but I wasn't very eager to let people know that I was only ACH/WS* – the equivalent of a general labourer! This was a far cry from tailoring and I was beginning to wonder how many more doors were going to be slammed in my face.

I moved my kit and belongings into my new billet where I was to share a room with three others. One of them was Gwen and she, too, was leaving Parachute Section. Once again I was on the ground floor but this time with the added luxury of a chest of drawers and a chair!

* ACH/WS = Aircraft hand/workshop.

Chapter 5

Fire-watching

ELECTRICAL and Wireless Technology (E. & W.T.) workshop was in complete contrast to the Parachute Section. The tall dark building was humming with activity. There were rows of benches each side of a central gangway and odd-looking pieces of machinery creating noise and a general atmosphere of industry. Everyone seemed to be engrossed in the work they were doing.

The whole section was divided into subsections and each sub-section was controlled by an N.C.O. He, in turn, was responsible to the Warrant Officer. The airmen who worked here were nearly all qualified electricians. This was one of the few trades that was spread over two pay scale grades. Electrician II was in Grade II and the R.A.F. course of learning took four months and if the airman passed this examination he was given 'his trade'. He could then go on to sit for his first class and then for Leading Aircraftmanship. Once having achieved this standard he was then eligible to sit for Electrician I, which was in Grade I and carried a higher degree of skill and know-how. Although the W.A.A.F. helped in the work there was no such trade open to women. They were ordinary workshop hands and came under Grade V.

There was plenty of work to be done, either modification on obsolete equipment or repairing broken electrical parts of aircraft such as generators, magnetos, switches, etc.

The six of us reported for duty and we were taken to the workshop stores and issued with thick navy overalls. Everything from stores was signed for and we were held responsible for whatever was drawn until it was returned. Each week we handed in our dirty overalls and received clean ones. We could borrow all kinds of tools and various pieces of equipment. Only tradesmen had their own tool kit for which they had to sign and no tradesmen would lend out tools.

Having donned my overall and settled in generally, I was given a heap of jettison switches used for releasing bomb loads. These were to be cleaned after dismantling, reassembled, painted and tested. There were hundreds of them. This salvage work was common in all walks of life during the war. Money was limited and so were supplies. The materials were needed urgently and this was the kind of work I would be doing.

The work was dirty and sometimes frustrating, but the job held something of a challenge. Nothing was thrown away and if a switch turned out to be useless the metal was salvaged and recycled. The same applied to other equipment and materials. I don't know how many hundreds of these switches I worked on but I was doing the job for some time, as were others. I was relieved when we came to the end of the batch and, eager to know what other work was expected from us; there was much to learn.

I think most of the airmen looked upon the WAAF as some sort of freaks. There were mixed feelings about whether they should or should not have been allowed to join the service. Most of them treated us with a cool respect but some, the odd few, thought our very existence intolerable and never ceased to remind us of it – "a woman's place is in the home", etc. They were entitled to their opinions. Working with the same airmen each day, it is not surprising we should prefer different company in the evening. Every so often a couple in the workshop would pair off for a date, but nothing serious. Most of the girls had boyfriends elsewhere.

There was one fellow I rather liked in E. & W.T. His name was Pat and he worked in Magneto Bay. I saw a lot of him at work and spoke to him often, but he never made dates with girls. I think he spent most of his spare time having a drink with the boys, I know he was always asking me for an aspirin! He was an Electrician II and seemed to be a very popular chap.

I was beginning to settle down in my new job and billet. I enjoyed the work and the friendly atmosphere of this particular bunch of people. Life was interesting and there was always something new to learn or talk about. News could be tragic too. Workmates would receive letters with news of a brother killed in action or a wife and children bombed out of their home and living in temporary accommodation. There were the "Dear John" letters and the parent, doing his duty as an air-raid warden, hurt by falling buildings, to mention a few of the happenings with which we had to learn to live.

We were all in the same boat and with no control whatsoever over the destiny of our loved ones. We all tried so hard to make the best of what little time we had. All of us wanted to get the war over, no one believing for one minute that the outcome would be any different from the way it was.

Posters were put up everywhere advising people not to talk about their work or any kind of military movement as enemy agents could be listening. We were warned to trust no one with any kind of information the enemy could make use of. Even the slightest hint could perhaps give the enemy the vital piece of information they were looking for. Once outside the workshop lips were sealed. If someone should want to talk shop there was always another who would give him a nudge and change the subject.

I expect I had been in E. & W.T. for about three months and, on this particular night, Gwen and I had arranged to go to the cinema in Llantwit. After seeing the film we decided to catch the bus back to the unit. It was very dark and we weren't keen on the idea of walking back to camp. We got to the village square where the bus was in and waiting to leave. It was almost 10pm. By the side of the bus stop was a public house with a built in brick seat adjoining the outside wall. On the seat was an airman who appeared to be asleep. We nudged him to tell him the bus was about to leave and, as we did so, he fell forward as though he was completely lifeless. We both bent over to pick him up and, as we did so, could smell that he had been drinking. We managed to get him to his feet and told him again that the bus was leaving. He mumbled something incoherent and we went to board the bus. The poor chap fell flat on his face. We couldn't leave him in that condition so we decided to walk him between us back to camp. By then the bus had left.

Gwen grabbed one arm and I the other. Between us we managed to manoeuvre him forward. It wasn't easy and he kept yelling that his leg hurt him and then his foot. He seemed to be putting one foot in front of the other with no bother, so we carried on. All the way back he was talking of someone named Mabel and rambled on about his head hurting. The language he used was foul and we really couldn't make head or tail of what he was trying to say. Again and again he yelled for Mabel and we assumed it must have been the barmaid in the pub. He swore again about his foot hurting and how his head ached. Gwen and I were glad to see the gates of 32 M.U. It hadn't been an easy walk and he wasn't very willing. Once we got him to the gate we handed him over to the gate guard and explained how we had found him and brought him home.

We carried on, booked in and thought no more about him. We talked next day at work wondering if any other boys had heard him go into the billet. We would have liked to know how he managed from the Guard Room.

During the afternoon the tannoy blared out something – I couldn't hear with all the noise around me. Half an hour later the same message came over again. This time everyone seemed to hear it. It was a call "for the two waafs who walked an airman home from the village last night" to report at once to the Guard Room. Gwen and I looked at each and wondered what we had done wrong. We were dismissed by the sergeant and went to see what all this was about. We were more than surprised when we were questioned about everything that had been said on the way back from the village. Notes were taken of our name, rank, and number our billet address and workshop. Over and over again we were asked what was said. We told them all we could remember including the swear words.

It was then that we were told the airman was suffering from concussion and a broken ankle! He was in hospital quite ill. We didn't know what to say. We had walked that poor man about a couple of miles. We were also asked if he mentioned any name apart from Mabel. For some reason the R.A.F. police thought that he had been taken out that evening by some person or persons for the purpose of getting him drunk and to try to make him talk about his work. He was working on some very confidential equipment at the time. The R.A.F. police finally told us to go. We walked back to work stunned, as we just couldn't believe the whole thing had happened. We were to report again to the police if we should remember anything, however small, that we hadn't told them, but we remembered nothing more than we had already said.

Some weeks later that very same airman came into the workshop asking to speak to us. He thanked us for getting him back to camp that night and told us he had been posted. This really brought the war home to us and made us realise that the fighting was going on under our noses as well as abroad.

Everyone seemed to put on weight after a few weeks in the service and I was no exception. I don't know whether it was the stodgy food, change of environment or just a healthy appetite. I was finding my tunic more difficult to button up each day. Exercise was what I needed to get rid of some of those extra pounds. I had noticed one or two bicycles on camp ridden by ordinary personnel and wondered if there was a chance that I could have mine sent from home.

Usually we all paraded everywhere. After breakfast it was the duty of the N.C.O. in charge of the section to call us out of the dining hall and form a squad to march down to the workshop. This was all right because we all arrived at work about the same time but going to meals was a different matter. We were dismissed outside the dining hall and then it was a race to get to the servery to try to avoid a queue. As each squad arrived simultaneously a queue could not be avoided.

Once again, I thought that if I had a bike I'd probably be halfway through my dinner before the squads arrived. I made enquiries at the orderly room. I was given permission to have my cycle on camp with no bother. I made the necessary arrangements and it arrived a few days later. It was a semi racing type of bike and had a fixed wheel. My father had given me a bell to put on it when I was at home. It was the biggest bell I had ever seen and, in fact, it was so heavy that I had to have it fixed to the stem of the handlebars. To have it put on the handlebars in the usual way might have upset my balance. The bell caused a great deal of interest when the bike arrived. I cycled everywhere and this gave me much more leisure time too. I lost my excess weight and felt much better.

One day Pat came over to me and told me he had a dental appointment and asked if he could borrow my bike to go to the dentist. Of course I agreed but warned him about the fixed wheel. He grinned at me – I think he thought I was joking. He was back about an hour or so later and I hardly recognised him. He had a bump on his head and his nose. His chin was all scratched and his hand all grazed. He'd taken a nosedive over the handlebars caused by the fixed wheel, so he said. He wasn't sure how the fall came about – he only knew he was going downhill fast! He thanked me and said he would walk the next time. That, I thought, was the end of a beautiful friendship and I was rather disheartened by it.

I did meet and date one fellow who thought I was wonderful. He was from hutted camp and we met at a dance in the gym. He was on the flight mechanics course and had only a few more weeks to go before leaving. He was Irish and 10 years my senior. We met several times and he took me to the cinema and for walks. Nothing special, but he was amusing and I enjoyed listening to his Irish brogue. A week or so before he was due to be posted we were out walking, and quite suddenly, he asked me to marry him! I had no idea his feelings were running so deeply. I liked him, but that was all. I didn't know what to say, so I told him I wasn't ready for marriage yet. He didn't mind and said he'd wait. I tried to laugh it off but he was serious, very serious. I'd never seen him like this before. I then told him I didn't think we should see each other again. He was most upset and said he would wait at the usual place the following night and begged me to be there. I said goodnight to him and reluctantly he left me. I didn't go to meet him the next night as I thought it best not to linger with our farewell. He was due for posting almost anytime and we were going to say "good-bye" anyway.

Doris had been seeing a friend of his who was on the same course and she came in the next day with a message from Paddy asking me to meet him just once more before he left. I explained to Doris what had happened between us and asked what she would do in my shoes. She agreed with me so I decided not to go to see him.

It was Thursday night when I last heard from him. A message came through to the billet telling me there was someone at the gate asking for me. As it was a domestic night I couldn't get out of camp. Anyway I thought he was overdoing things a bit. I didn't go to the gate and I never saw him again. I have often wondered about him since. My first proposal of marriage and I wasn't even starry-eyed!

I had the odd date here and there after that, but nothing serious. I was still under 18 but growing fast! At least I thought I was! Jock, an electrician in Mag Bay was telling me one day how beautiful it was in Wick. He described the place in great detail and I was impressed. I happened to mention this to Ian, a young Welsh boy from the valleys, and he told me that Wick wasn't far from where he lived. I was surprised, and told him I'd like to visit the place, so he gave me details of the bus route and service.

The following Saturday afternoon Gwen and I set out for Wick. The bus took us out in the country for some miles through all the little Welsh villages with their peculiar names. I had no idea in which way we were going. The bus twisted and turned down the narrow lanes and then the conductor told us that our stop was next. When we went to get off the bus we could only see a couple of cottages. The conductor assured us that this was Wick. We started to look for the shops and came to a small general store – that was all! There were very few houses and the place looked very much like a tiny hamlet. We called in the shop and asked again. Yes, this was Wick. We were in the middle of nowhere on a Saturday afternoon! Not only that, but it was a two hour wait for a bus to take us back. Poor old Gwen – I had asked her to come with me, thinking we were going to have a whale of a time. By the time we got back to St Athan it was too late to do anything or go anywhere.

I had been deliberately misled and I got a bit steamed up about it. Jock had omitted to tell us that he had been describing Wick in Scotland, and Ian laughed his head off. I was learning the hard way!

Fire-watching was a duty performed by all W.A.A.F. personnel. It was an all-night job and nobody liked it although there was really nothing to it. It came around about every second week and it always varied a bit and we were never sure when we would be called upon. We were informed by the orderly from the orderly room. He would come around to the workshop with his roster and give us the date and place of the next duty. We had to sign in his little book to confirm that we had been told. That way there was no question of anyone "forgetting". We were usually given 48 hours' notice. Two of us were always on duty at the same time and we very seldom did fire-watching with the same person twice. We were allowed to leave off work an hour early on that particular day and get an early tea. The fire-watching started at 6pm so we had to be back to the workshop by then and not always at the same workshop either.

Our duty was to keep an eye open for fires starting should there be a raid or even sabotage. We never did encounter either, but the duty had to be performed just the same. There were usually two beds somewhere in the office of each workshop, which were used expressly for this purpose. It was always advisable to wake early the following morning otherwise it was possible to be caught in bed with everyone coming in to work at 7.30! We had to leave the office as we found it, get a late breakfast and have a couple of hours off before reporting back to work. Although the whole thing was a bind it was a good time to catch up with our letter writing and any mending we might have to do.

One night I was on duty fire-watching with a girl I didn't know very well. Her name was Dora and she worked in the dope* shop. It was a dirty night, cold and blowing a gale with rain coming down like stair rods. We settled down for the night to the rattle of the creaking of the building. I don't know what time it was, but I had to get up, as I wanted to go to the toilet. I put my battledress over my pyjamas, put my great coat over that and set forth. It was pitch black outside with the rain and wind competing with each other. I had 500 yards to go to get to the nearest toilet. I wanted to go so badly and I hadn't a torch. Half asleep, I stood hesitating in the doorway – not only was I going to get a soaking, but I was going to get lost as well, if I weren't careful, as it was so dark out there. Then my eye caught the row of fire buckets just inside the doorway filled ready for use. I decided to use one of them instead. I'd never done anything like that before, but as long as I emptied, washed and refilled it in the morning, I could see no harm in it. That was my intention.

The next morning we were awakened by the men coming into the gun turrets section to start work. We had overslept! What a scramble we had in getting dressed, making our beds and collecting together our bits and pieces. There was no time to wash or clean the fire bucket! I said nothing to Dora. Whether she had heard me get up in the night I really don't know. I had to make a quick decision –

---

* Dope was the slang word used for a kind of waterproof paint used to seal rubber dinghies.

either empty the bucket in front of everyone or leave it and trust no one would notice it. I left it.

I returned to work and I hadn't been there long when the sergeant told me I was wanted in the office. When I got there I was asked if I had been fire-watching the night before and, if so, where. My heart was in my mouth. Surely no one had found out about the bucket? I was asked to report to the Squadron Leader of gun turrets. He asked us who had fouled the fire bucket. I was so ashamed and so terribly embarrassed that I couldn't bring myself to answer. Dora was disgusted, and stated quite clearly that this didn't concern her and then stormed off. I was literally shaking in my shoes. I waited to hear what was coming next. Very quietly the officer told me that the fire buckets had been fouled many times before and he didn't think it was fair that

With friends outside our billet, Kidbrooke – summer 1943.

63

his men should have the job of cleaning and refilling them. He thought it only right that I should clean the one that I had fouled – he also told me that everyone in the workshop knew what I had done. I then had to go down into the workshop, fetch the fire bucket, take it to the ablutions, wash it out, fill it and return it.

If my face was red before, I think it must have been scarlet now right down to my knees. I staggered the length of gun turrets carrying the bucket of water. The boys were whistling and calling things to me. That was bad enough but when I took the thing back it was even worse! I can remember almost every second of that journey, as never, in my whole life, have I ever felt quite so embarrassed as I was then. I kept clear of fire buckets after that whatever the weather!

Chapter 6

Electrician II

THERE was always someone going on leave in the section. We were granted seven days every three months and this was underlined as a privilege. Any leave pass could be cancelled without notice at any time, so it was wise not to count too much on leave, and never take it for granted. Forty-eight hour passes were usually granted every four to six weeks according to the pressure of the station. I had a pass due to me and I didn't quite know how to use it. Gwen suggested she took hers at the same time and we could go somewhere together. I thought this was a good idea. The boys were always coming back from their week-ends off saying that they had hitchhiked home and some of them lived as far away as Brighton and Birmingham. I asked Gwen if she fancied trying to hitchhike home – she lived at Seaford in Sussex. She was willing to have a try so we went ahead with arrangements.

We asked the boys if they could give us some tips for our weekend. The only suggestion that was forthcoming was the same from each of them. The best way to get a lift to London was to get on the main Cardiff road as early as poss-ible. We decided to take with us as little as possible so I put a clean collar and a toothbrush in my respirator case and some pipe cleaner curlers in my pocket.

We got our passes on the Friday afternoon. We didn't

stop for tea but went straight out of camp as the boys had advised us to do. We got on the road and started to walk. There didn't seem to be much traffic about at all. The weather was fine but not especially warm. The walking kept our blood circulation going. We walked and we walked. The odd truck and service car was all we saw but they didn't stop and we were beginning to despair as we weren't going to get home that night for sure. We were getting tired and hungry not having eaten since midday. It was now 9.30pm and we'd been walking most of the way since we left. We decided to try and find somewhere to sleep. It wasn't easy. There wasn't a light in sight because of the blackout. We couldn't tell if we were near a built–up area or not. In the end we thought the best thing to do was to find a piece of sheltered ground somewhere and try to sleep. It was late March and although the weather wasn't particularly cold it wasn't very warm either.

We could see what we thought was some heathland and made our way over to it. We stumbled into a clump of bushes and that was where we stayed. I put my curlers in, loosened my collar wrapped my greatcoat around me and used my respirator as a pillow. The ground was hard and not at all comfortable. We eventually fell asleep.

We woke early next morning, very stiff and not in the least refreshed. We both felt chilly although it was a bright morning. I combed my hair and fixed it in a band to keep it tidy, straightened my collar and brushed myself down the best I could. Gwen and I checked each other to make sure we were presentable, and we started off again searching for somewhere to wash. We weren't far from a village, only a small place – Dinas Powis we learned later

There in a wall on the edge of the village square was a tap with an ornamental bowl beneath it – just the ideal place for a wash. The water was cold and refreshing. We scrubbed our teeth and felt a lot better. There was no one about, in fact the place looked deserted. It was 6am.

Our original plans had long been abandoned. Our only goal now was to get something to eat and a place to sleep for the night. We made for the road again. To our surprise an ambulance came by and the driver stopped and asked us if we would like a lift into Cardiff. He said, he was on his way to work. We didn't ride far before he dropped us off. Neither of us realised we had been so close to the city. We thanked the driver and he drove off. We made for the nearest place for a meal.

After we had eaten our first job was to make sure of a bed that night. It was Saturday and the Y.M.C.A. might already be booked up. We found a phone box and gave them a ring. Our luck was in as they had a bed for each of us. As Gwen came out of the phone box she pressed Button B and several pennies dropped out. We had to giggle and, as we walked along, we tried Button B in another box and two pennies fell out. This was money for nothing! Each phone box we saw that day we did the same and ended up nearly two shillings better off!

We spent the rest of the day looking around Cardiff. We saw a film, had another meal and decided to call it a day. We appreciated the bed we had booked. We were exhausted and slept well. Next morning, after breakfast, we went straight to the station and caught the first train back to camp. I had already decided that hitchhiking was not for me and I had no intention of trying it again.

On Monday when we got into work we learned that the 'main Cardiff road' which we had been advised to use was on the other side of Cardiff! I suppose my own common sense should have told me that and Gwen and I were the talking point for days afterwards. It was a long while before we lived that one down.

At work my job was getting more and more interesting as I was now working on generators – dismantling and cleaning them using a lathe to skim the commutators and servicing them in general. Help was always there when needed and the boys were usually most co-operative. The section Warrant Officer seemed to have a soft spot for us girls and went out of his way to see that we were well looked after. Now and then he would come around the workshop to have a chat with everyone. I think he gained the confidence of all of us. He had spent most of his life in the R.A.F. and he wasn't a young man. His name was Smith.

We had been working in E. & W.T. for about eight months when the sergeant came and told us that we were wanted by W.O. Smith in his office. The six of us wondered what kind of news awaited us. We all thought we were off again to another workshop.

Smithy, as we called him, was all smiles. He ushered us in and sat and looked at us. It seemed ages before he spoke and then, when he did speak, he surprised the lot of us. He said he had a plan and he needed our co-operation – we were intrigued. He went on to say how pleased he was with the job we were doing and he liked the way we had knuckled down to it and was pleased with the progress we had made since we had been there, but, he said, that wasn't enough and he wanted us to learn about electricity. In return he would try to get the trade opened for us and if he were successful, we would be able to sit for a trade board, and with a bit of luck and learning, we should be able to become electricians. Needless to say we were open-mouthed and completely speechless. He asked us what we thought about the idea but none of us could speak. He then asked us if we would be willing to learn in the evenings, which would mean giving up some of our free time, but he couldn't say more. We all agreed that we would like to try to do what we could. Smithy rubbed his hands and said we could go. He had to see what he could do about getting us a teacher who was as willing as we were. We left his office and went back to the bench. I don't think any of us did much work for the rest of that day and we couldn't stop talking about the possibilities of our becoming electricians. Most of the boys in the shop thought the whole idea was utterly ridiculous. How could women expect to learn, in a few evenings, a job which had taken them every day of four months? So the argument went on. None of us girls had any idea of how much there was to learn, but we were all eager to give it a try, and if we failed we had lost nothing.

It was not long before Smithy called us together again and this time he told us he had managed to borrow a lecture room. He said, that as for teachers, we would have to be content with those he could get and when they could get there. This all sounded a bit up in the air to us but we were still game. I think Smithy was trying to realise a pipe dream. We were given notebooks and told to furnish ourselves with more if needed. He was depending on us helping ourselves in any way possible.

In less than a week we were having our first lecture which

was given by another Warrant Officer whom we'd never seen before and he lectured us quite a lot. We also had Flight Sergeants and Sergeants of E. & W.T. explaining different things to us. We were given circuits and various other papers to help us. After two weeks we had a written test. It was very simple but covered a great deal of ground. The results of this pleased Smithy. We continued to learn and we had no idea how long we would be attending these classes but we went on as long as Smithy asked us.

Nearly two months had passed since our first lecture and we were informed that we had to sit a Board for our Electrician Trade Test. This was to be held in Sealand somewhere up near Chester. Smithy also told us he had spent a lot of money on drink trying to persuade the powers that be that his girls were capable of passing the test! We all hoped that we wouldn't let him down but we weren't very sure of ourselves.

The day came for us to go to Sealand. We were to travel up one day, stay the night, have our board the next day and then back to St Athan. None of us gave much for our chances, but we kept that to ourselves. The boys in the shop wished us well but I think they felt the same as us.

We didn't know the results right away. We had to wait for them to come through the usual channels. It didn't take long. One morning Smithy came striding down the shop waving a piece of paper in his hand and grinning all over his face. "We've done it," he said. "We've done it." We knew he'd got the results of the trade board and that we had passed. We could hardly believe it. Smithy was so proud. He told us we would go down in R.A.F. history as the first six waafs ever to pass the trade test board for electricians.

"Now," he said, "you'll get paid the proper wage for the job." We did too! We were upgraded to Grade II and, before many weeks had gone by, we sat and passed our First Class. Within six months of us getting our trade we were all 'Leading Aircraftswomen Electrician II' and that was as high as we could go. Later the trade was opened to all W.A.A.F. personnel. I'd been in the service for just 12 months but it seemed like a lifetime since those days in the clothing factory.

With our trade behind us our job seemed to be that much simpler. We now understood why we did or did not do certain things with certain equipment. We were well aware of the action of the pieces we were repairing. We listened with interest when arguments cropped up at work. It was fun too, to be able to play the old trick on someone else with the Megger.

Electricians working in the armoury were under pressure – with so much work to do they needed some help. I was sent in for a few weeks to give them a hand. There were only five fellows in that particular sub-section and they worked on bomb release equipment. I sat most of the day soldering on tiny tags. The job was cleaner and simpler than with generators. The fellows I worked with were pleasant and I got on well with them.

I shared a bench with Dai – he was of course, a Welsh-man. He lived not far from Newport and was able to get home frequently. He was always singing off key but insisted he was in the choir at home. We used to have quite a few laughs. He was engaged to a girl at home.

He had been on leave and had only been back for a day or two when I decided to wire up his toolbox to the Megger.

The others thought this was hilarious and a wonderful idea. I got the thing all set up and when Dai went to unlock his toolbox in the morning I gave the Megger a couple of turns which gave Dai an electric shock. He yelled out a string of swear words in Welsh and then proceeded to call me everything he could lay his tongue to. At the time I thought it a huge joke and the other boys were curled up laughing, but I didn't know Dai very well. Apparently he couldn't take a joke when it was on him, and although I was working only two feet away from him he refused to speak to me. At first I thought it was because he was mad at me, so I let it ride all that day. The next day when I said "Good morning" to him, he ignored me completely. I still took no notice but every hour or so I would ask him for something or other and he acted as though I wasn't there. I didn't try after that. The whole thing upset me and I couldn't tell anyone why. I even went off my food. I couldn't eat for days and the other girls were getting quite worried about me. I think it was five days before I ate anything. The girls tried to tempt me with their chocolate rations but even that didn't work. I felt I just couldn't get it past my lips. Eventually, of course I did begin to eat, very little at first and then normally.

Dai did speak to me later but very grudgingly. I think he must have hated the very air I breathed. If I'd known he was going to react so violently I would never have attempted such a silly thing on him. Maybe it was because he had just got back from leave. I don't know but I would never forget. I worked on the section for four months only and then returned to E. & W.T. I never wired anyone else to the Megger although I had it done to me several times.

When I went back to my old shop I was put into a

different sub-section. I worked on hand magnetos, simple little things but tricky. Gwen was working with me as well and we were under a corporal this time. This section was very small with only two waafs and two airmen. I still had this sneaky liking for Pat and he seemed to be pleased to see me back. He would sometimes come over and chat to me.

Gwen and I still went around together and sometimes another couple more would join us. We all made arrangements to go over to hutted camp to see a film one night and as usual, we had to queue for the second house. There was no chance of seeing the film around twice because they cleared the cinema after each performance.

While we were waiting who should give me a poke in the back but Pat. We chatted a bit and then he asked me if he could take me into the cinema. I didn't want to leave the girls but they insisted that they didn't mind. I didn't want to say "no" to Pat but I couldn't understand why he hadn't asked me properly instead of waiting until I was in other company. He knew all the girls as well as he knew me. He told me later in the evening that he had intended to ask me out but then he heard the girls talking and learned I had already arranged to go with them. I still don't know why he couldn't have waited until the next night or any other night. Anyway, we saw the film and he walked me back to camp. He asked me to meet him a couple of nights later and go to hutted camp cinema and see a different film. I agreed.

We met for our date and chatted freely as we walked around the perimeter. As we were talking I thought I felt his arm slide around my waist. I edged away and he looked at me oddly as I told him that there was a time and place for everything. He strongly denied the action. Then, as I was walking along I could feel my little French panties gradually slipping down. Then I realised that I had felt the elastic in them giving way! I didn't know what to do. If I kept walking then the panties would just fall to the ground. I couldn't ignore them. Once the elastic was broken there was nothing to keep them up! I asked Pat to keep on walking and not to look around. I'm sure he must have thought I was mad, to say the least. He walked on and I sedately stepped out of my underwear. I picked up my panties and rolled them in a ball in my hand. I had to say something so I told him what had happened. I was so embarrassed that I didn't know what I was doing. He laughed and offered to put them in his pocket! I didn't feel so bad then and we carried on and enjoyed the rest of the evening. It was a bit cool walking back that night! We began to date regularly after that.

Reading D.R.O.s one day I was surprised to see that all W.A.A.F. personnel were to be issued with steel truncheons. This caused a lot of speculation. We were not told why these were being issued and nor were we told how to or when to use them. The truncheon was about 14 inches long and weighed 7 pounds. It was to be worn at all times, hanging from the hook on our respirator case. To carry this as well as a respirator and tin helmet was no mean feat. Airmen were not issued with them, but they were ordered to carry Sten guns instead.

We carried these about with us for about a month. No one seemed to know why. Wild stories were told of a forthcoming invasion and some tales were so ridiculous that it was hard to imagine what the truth could be. I know that several of our airmen landed in hospital with cracked skulls!

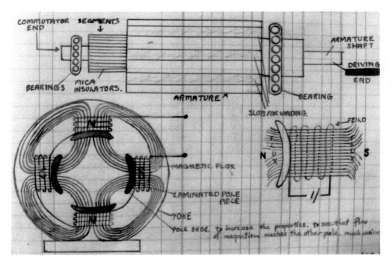

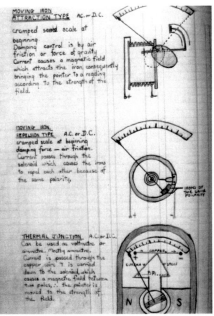

Copies of Notes and Circuits taken from my Gen Book – on exhibition at Flixton Airport Museum.

75

The only reasonable story I heard was that prisoners had escaped from a nearby prisoner of war camp. It was believed they may have tried to get a R.A.F. uniform from personnel outside the camp because their prison clothes were easy to identify. This would have enabled them to approach aircraft and perhaps flee the country.

I am still unaware of the true facts but, after the said month or so, truncheons were withdrawn and conditions went back to normal.

Chapter 7

Dried Egg and Foreigners

CORPORAL Gulley was in charge of the little sub-section of hand magnetos where I worked with Gwen and one other airman. Although we all knew his name was Ted he insisted on being called Corporal Gulley. He was a bit of a stinker. He was from somewhere in London and I think he'd lived in most places, as he seemed to know everything. He was about 23 years old and very smart. Instead of the usual service mug that everyone was issued with, he had a fine pewter mug which he regarded very highly and it was kept upside down on his work locker.

Gwen and I didn't care much for Corporal Gulley, but of course we had to do his bidding. He was one of the few who thought the service was no place for women. He had been particularly nasty with us one day and both of us wanted to do something to irritate him without getting ourselves into trouble. We thought about it for a bit, but could think of nothing until my eyes settled on his mug! With no further thought, while he was out of the section, I put a hole in the bottom with a pin, not big enough to notice when empty but he would surely notice it when full. We sat back and waited.

The N.A.A.F.I. wagon came around as usual in the afternoon and out went Corporal Gulley; mug in hand, to get his tea. We went to get ours as well but kept an eye open for Ted. We had our break in the workshop because of the inclement weather and he sat in his usual place. We saw him look at the base of his mug and wipe it with a piece of cotton waste. We tried to behave normally. Again he wiped the base of his mug and also the bench where it was standing. Gwen and I stifled a giggle and we waited for whatever was to come next.

Strangely enough he didn't seem unduly ruffled. He finished his tea and as he did so, tipped his mug upside down and let the last few drops fall on the floor. He then held his mug up to the light and peered into the bottom of it. We nudged each other and got on with our work.

Next thing we noticed was Corporal Gulley heating a soldering iron. We were expecting him to be hopping mad by now but he was calmly filling up the hole with solder. When he had finished he put the mug back in its usual place.

This wasn't good enough as he hadn't appeared to be at all irritated. We thought for a while, and then I told Gwen I was going to do it again. As soon as his back was turned I pierced another hole in his precious mug and replaced it exactly as before. We wouldn't be able to see the outcome of this one because the next time he used it would be in the dining hall and the men ate separately from the women. We could only wait until morning and see if he used the soldering iron again.

Next morning, as usual up went his mug on his locker and out came the soldering iron! He turned and asked each of us if we had seen anyone come into the section the previous afternoon. We told him we had seen no one and asked why he was enquiring.

78

He said it didn't matter. He repaired his mug with more difficulty than the last time and, as he did so, I went over to him and asked what he was doing. He told me about the two holes. It was hard for me to keep a straight face. I commiserated with him.

We were still surprised to see how placid he was. Perhaps we weren't upsetting him as much as we thought. To add insult to injury I put a third hole in his mug. This did the trick. If he wasn't mad before he certainly was mad then. I think he would have strangled me freely if he had known I was the culprit. He swore and went ahead like a mad thing. He was livid. He repaired the mug again and said no more.

For days afterwards he seemed a bit uneasy. I felt terribly sorry for what I had done and wanted desperately to apologise. I told Gwen how I felt and she laughed and told me not to be so stupid but I couldn't leave things as they were. I had made up my mind that I was going to tell him and apologise. I picked a moment when I thought he wasn't very busy. I was expecting him to swear at me, or something like that, but he didn't. In fact he hugged me! He told me he was quite relieved to know who it was and even thanked me for telling him. After that we all got on fine together. I think we both gained the respect of the other from that experience.

With war in its third year and no end in sight, restrictions and rationing had crept into everything. Travel was limited, our beaches were sealed off and some of them mined as a defence against invasion. Troops were constantly seen in convoy and large areas of the countryside were fenced off and guarded, sometimes defending an airfield or a secret hideout, or just a practise bombing or shooting range. Whisky, gin and other drinks were allocated to public houses in very limited quantities. Petrol was rationed and sweets and cigarettes were in short supply. Paper was salvaged and re-cycled so many times that it was difficult to buy a writing pad containing pure white leaves. Everything was packed in utility wrappings if packed at all. Polythene and plastics had not come on the scene. What few books were published and printed were of inferior paper and covers. Colours and decorations were luxuries we could ill afford. Eggs had been dehydrated and were being sold in powder form. Saccharin took the place of sugar in most edible things. Even furniture was limited and the newlyweds had to get dockets for any furniture they needed and these were issued only for the bare necessities. All household linen was rationed and coupons also had to be surrendered before buying clothes. Some liked to buy clothes more frequently than others so there was a ready market for clothing coupons.

A black market existed for most things provided the money was cash. High wages were being earned by factory workers as they worked long hours to keep up production figures. With everything in short supply there wasn't much on which to spend their money. Television sets, refrigera-tors, washing machines, etc had not yet reached the homes of the average citizen and so were not available. Quality make-up was hard to find but there were others on the market, some of which I'm sure were made of lard! Perfume was very rarely seen in the shops and when it was, we had to be careful when using it. Some of it burned holes in clothes or discoloured them and they didn't smell all that good either. If a retailer should be lucky enough to receive a quota of any reputable cosmetics he only had to sell one and the women would queue for hours until his stock was exhausted. It was a question of first come, first served – but not always. After a while, a lot of stuff was being 'put under the counter'. This meant that the retailer would sell only to customers whom he chose. Fiddles and confidence tricks were rife. People began to long for just the tiniest luxury just to break the monotony. A whisper in the ear from someone who had something to sell and the money was there – no questions asked. Often it was bought unseen, only to find later it was a load of rubbish. So we were educated to a new way of life.

From time to time each of us in the billet received from home a parcel of 'goodies'. Not much perhaps, but it cheered us and we always shared with those immediately around us. Home-made cakes we scoffed at one sitting and home-brewed tea was indeed a luxury.

I had received a parcel from home and in it was a box of powdered egg. I'd never had the stuff before so I put it aside for later. I shared out the other contents as usual. Next day at work I mentioned to Pat about the powdered egg. He told me his mother used it often and went ahead to explain how. It all sounded very simple. Just mix with water to a stiff batter and fry. I promised to make him some. Not having done much cooking before I had my tongue in cheek and fingers crossed! He gave me his mess can, a small collapsible pan used in emergencies for meals in the field. It was part of his kit and was polished to a very high standard. Of course he'd never had the need to use it.

I waited for domestic night because that was the only time we had an open fire in the billet. There were other means for cooking. I arranged to see Pat at 9pm outside the N.A.A.F.I. where I would give him his powdered egg supper. Having made all the arrangements there was only the cooking left to do. I followed the instructions on the packet and proceeded to fry the egg in Pat's mess pan, as I had nothing else to use. I had no fat and only an open fire. The whole thing was a complete mess. His pan was blackened by the coal, his egg cooked but when I tried to turn it over with my knife to cook the other side the whole thing broke into pieces.

The girls were watching me with great interest. I had loads of advice, all of which was totally unacceptable. I couldn't let Pat down now as he was probably looking forward to a home-cooked supper and already waiting by the N.A.A.F.I. I took him the egg in the mess can. He didn't recognise the pan at all and, thank goodness, it was too dark to see the contents. He didn't stop but hurried to his billet to eat his supper while it was still hot!

Next day I didn't want to know what he thought of his egg supper, as I felt a bit sensitive about it. I said nothing but waited to hear what he had to say – if anything. It was some days later when the subject cropped up. He told me he had spent two hours cleaning his mess can! Not a mention of the egg. I went off dried eggs after that but Pat didn't go off me!

We continued to see quite a lot of each other and most nights he would ask me to go out with him somewhere. His home was in Monmouth – a small town in the Wye Valley. He was able to get home at weekends if he wanted, but he only went home when he could get a 48-hour pass. There were times when I wished I could get home too, if only to have a natter with my sisters. They were growing up so fast and each time I went home I could see a difference in them. I had their letters of course.

Kit had left the silk factory and was now putting the buttonholes in khaki battledress for the same firm as I had worked for just prior to joining up. Eileen, my younger sister, was working on a sewing machine at the silk factory. She was still at school when I left home. Marie, my youngest sister, was still at school. She hated the air raids and was terrified of the sound of the guns and the aircraft overhead. Young Michael was not yet at school so he didn't realise the seriousness of it all. He didn't seem worried about anything.

My father was an air raid warden in his spare time. Each time the 'Alert' sounded he had to go on duty outside in the streets, making sure that everyone was under cover and to keep a look out for lights and incendiaries. It wasn't very pleasant for him or my mother. He was at risk most of the time. He had left his job as a bus driver and was then working for the civil defence full-time. His main task was salvaging personal property for people who had been bombed out.

My mother had to rouse everyone in the house and hasten them to the air-raid shelters whenever there was a raid in the night. My sisters sometimes preferred to stay in bed but this was a worry to my mother and Marie, who was so frightened. By the time they were all back in bed again it was time to get up. As the air raids became more frequent some people didn't go to bed but went down into their air raid shelter and slept there. At least their rest wasn't disturbed and that was a big thing when everyone was working such long hours. Surprisingly enough they seemed to keep healthy.

I wrote home regularly and told them about the films I

had seen and if I had been anywhere special. We weren't allowed to tell about the work or camp in letters so news was kept to a more personal level. I told my parents I was going out with Pat. I had never told them when I had been out with a boy before so they probably thought he was the first one! I didn't dare tell them about my panties falling down!

It was February 1943 when Pat asked me to visit his home and meet his parents. I was thrilled to bits at the idea but also very apprehensive. We made plans for the following weekend. We managed to get away from the camp early on the Saturday and caught the train to Newport where we had to change to the local train that ran through the Wye Valley to Troy Station in Monmouth. It was a pretty journey and Pat pointed out places of interest such as Tintern Abbey, etc. His 15-year-old brother was at the station to meet us, and we walked the half mile to Pat's home where his parents and his elder sisters were waiting for us and made us most welcome. We had a good long chat over a cup of tea. Pat's mother was Welsh, his father was a Scot and I found them very pleasant and easy to talk to.

Teatime came and we all took our places at the table except Pat's young sister Anne. She was a year younger than me and was upstairs getting ready to meet me, so I learned afterwards. At last she came down and we began to eat. Each time I looked up Anne was looking at me. It was as if she couldn't take her eyes off me and she didn't say a word. I was beginning to feel a bit embarrassed. Then her mother asked her if she wanted something to eat. I think that broke the spell and she didn't look quite so hard at me after that. The meal was enjoyable and they really made me feel at home. His mother told me later that she had two more sons – one away in the army and a younger one in the Air Force. Pat had never mentioned them to me. When tea was over we four women went into the kitchen to wash the dishes. While we were washing up, Anne apologised for being late down to tea and explained she had been trying to do something with the back of her hair as it hadn't curled properly. She said she'd have another try at it when we had finished the dishes. She brought out an old-fashioned set of curling tongs and put them on the gas ring to heat. Although I had never used them myself I had often watched my grandmother use a set. When Anne thought they were hot enough she tested them on a piece of newspaper and satisfied they were not too hot, she proceeded to try to curl the back of her hair. She was finding the job a little difficult so I offered to help. I reheated the tongs and separated the piece of hair that was to be curled. Having done that I wrapped the hair around the hot tongs but I had forgotten to test them. I tried to pull the tongs away, but the lump of hair came away with them and was sizzling on the tongs! I didn't know whether to laugh or cry. I felt so awful. Anne was trying to conceal her feelings but I knew she must be furious. I know I would have been. I apologised but it didn't help matters at all. Anne put the tongs away and went upstairs. I didn't see her anymore that day.

It was time for Pat and me to leave, as we had to be back at camp by midnight. Although, we hadn't been long at his home I had enjoyed meeting his folks but I couldn't be sure they would say the same about me! I apologised again to his mother for spoiling Anne's hair. She told me not to worry, as Anne would soon forget it. We said our farewells and left.

On the way back Pat asked me to tell him what had happened to Anne's hair. I told him how dreadful I felt about the whole thing. He laughed his head off!

I spent many happy weekends with his sisters after that. I learned many of the tricks the girls were using in civvy street to combat the shortages. Stockings were in short supply and Pat's sisters always looked as though they could get plenty. They told me what they did to look so well dressed. They would first buy a bottle of gravy browning and cover their legs with it. If put on evenly it gave the legs the look of sheer nylon. Then they would get a black eyebrow pencil and make a line down the back of their legs to look like a seam! I asked them if the flies caused them any trouble, but they said the only thing they feared was that a dog might have a lick and so ruin the whole thing! Mascara was in short supply so shoe polish was used instead. Another time I was there they were getting ready to go to a dance in the evening. Shoes could not be bought without coupons and their supply was limited like everyone else's and if they hadn't got a pair of shoes the colour they required – then they painted a pair with ordinary household paint. One pair of shoes I know had been painted three times – each time a different colour.

'FOREIGNERS'

'Foreigners' was the name given to anything made in the workshop for ourselves. With all the equipment and tools at our disposal it was not surprising to see fellows using them to their own advantage. All sorts of little trinkets were shaped and fashioned to take home to the family. Cigarette lighters were made with copper coins sweated into the sides of a big brass nut; brooches were made with silver coins totally defaced to make a replica of a spitfire. These were just a couple of 'foreigners' that were popular at the time. Some airmen were more ambitious and made scale models of aircraft from scrap metal and perspex. These made centrepieces for tables and some were really handsome. All these were sent or taken home as gifts or sold to those who were not so dexterous. Artistry and imagination came from the most unexpected sources and everyone had to be careful not to get caught.

Pat had given me a snapshot of himself and it was very small. I wanted something a little bigger to put in the billet so I decided to make a large sketch of the snapshot. I didn't know anything about drawing and I just copied down his features with a pencil on paper. It wasn't a bad likeness so I took it into work and showed him. He was very impressed. As he was so interested I promised to send home and get one or two of the sketch copies I had made of film stars before I joined the service. I had always liked to draw and sketch even though I knew nothing about it and I'd never shown them to anyone before. I was rather pleased when so much interest was shown not only by Pat but by others as well. I had always thought that everyone could draw, the same as everyone could write. I had no idea I might have something special like drawing ability or talent.

After the 'oohs' and 'aahs' had died down and my drawings were back in the billet, one of the electricians came over to speak to me. Although I had seen the fellow around I had never spoken to him before. He asked me if I had ever been taught to sketch properly. I told him that the only art I had ever been taught was in class at school, drawing the odd buttercup or daffodil. He went on to say that, providing I was willing, he would teach me all I needed to know to become a commercial artist. I told him I would think about it, not realising what an opportunity I was being offered. I did think about it, but I had just spent all those weeks giving up my free time to be an electrician and Pat and I were going steady. As much as I would have liked to learn all I could I felt that this was not the time. I thanked him and declined his offer. Little did I realise that I might have turned down the chance of a lifetime. That very same electrician was a commercial artist in civvy street and a good one at that from what I heard later. He painted murals on the walls of the dining halls at St Athan and, although I didn't see them, I heard they were sensational.

Chapter 8

Kidbrooke

I was rather looking forward to my next leave. I always did, but this time it was special. I had asked my mother if I could take Pat home so that she could meet him, and she had agreed. I would have liked my father to have met him at the same time, but he had volunteered for the R.A.F. and was due to go to Cardington for his basic training. What had brought all this about I had no idea. He was 39 years old and in a reserved occupation. Pat was disappointed. He said, it was nerve racking enough having to meet them all, without having to go through it twice!

At last the day came for us to go on leave and we set off for Ipswich. Pat had travelled quite a bit before. He was a regular serviceman and five years my senior. He had been to Scotland and Yorkshire and had served with the 'Few' at Hornchurch during the Battle of Britain (as it was later called) but he had never been to Suffolk and was looking forward to seeing the old town of Ipswich.

We had decided to split our leave in two. It was natural for him to want to spend some time with his own family, so he decided that he would stay in Ipswich for four days and then go back to Monmouth on his own, leaving me to spend the rest of my leave with my family. We'd meet again when we got back to camp. In those four days, I showed him as much as I could of the town. It was much bigger than he had imagined and he loved Christchurch Park and The Mansion House.

My sisters fell for him in their own way and he was taken up with my young brother. My mother seemed to like him too and I was pleased about that. I hoped my father would like him. While I was home I asked my mother the reason why my father had joined up. She told me that he had thought about it for quite a while and, finally decided he could probably do more for his country in uniform than he was doing in civvy street. He was a conscientious man and I hoped he wouldn't be disillusioned.

The days slipped round all too quickly and the time came for Pat to go back to Monmouth. I went to see him off at the station and after he had gone, I was surprised to find how much I missed him. This was the first time we had been apart for weeks. We had been working together all day and going out with each other most nights. I hadn't realised how much I had come to rely on his company. I found myself looking forward to going back to camp! I knew I would see him the day after.

Once back at camp I learned that things had happened while I had been on leave. The chemist at Llantwit had managed to get in a stock of perfume and some of the girls had bought some. On wearing it for the first time two of them had become engaged! They both declared the perfume had special qualities. Gwen was telling me this when Doris came in and suggested I wore some of her perfume when I went to meet Pat. "Maybe you'll be the third!" Doris said. I put some of the potent liquid behind my ears. It did smell rather pleasant – it was called Gardenia. I secretly hoped it would work for me!

I met Pat as arranged and we took a stroll down to the sea. It was a warm spring evening and the war seemed miles away. On the way back we stopped at the Y.M.C.A. in the village for a sandwich and a mug of tea. As we walked slowly back to camp we talked about birthdays. Mine was due the following month and I would be 19. Quite suddenly Pat turned to me and said, "How would you like to get engaged on your birthday?" This was so unexpected that I could hardly believe it. I thought of the perfume and hesitated. Surely a dab of perfume, however exotic, couldn't turn a fellow's head to that extent. I dismissed the thought and Pat repeated his question.

All I could say at the time was "Yes". I was too excited to say anything else. As we walked on to camp I made up my mind to buy a bottle of Gardenia!

The girls were still awake when I arrived back at the billet and, when I told them of Pat's proposal I don't think they believed me – not at first anyway. This was excusable because I found it hard to believe myself. I was so thrilled, I wrote to my mother the next day and told her the good news. For some reason I didn't hear from her straight away. The next letter I had was from my father, warning me of the pitfalls of marriage in wartime. I think it was only written for my own good, but it didn't dampen my spirits a bit.

A couple of weeks later Pat and I went to Bridgend to choose a ring. There were so few to choose from and I think there were only about four in Pat's price range. I couldn't make my mind up which one to have and it wasn't because I didn't see anything I liked but I thought it was a lot of money to spend on something I probably wouldn't be able to wear much. It would get spoiled wearing it for work but Pat insisted, so I chose the ring I fancied. It was a neat setting of platinum with a diamond centre and very pretty. I was very pleased and proud of it.

Word soon got around that we were engaged and all sorts of things were said to us which when summed up, meant they all wished us well. Three days later I was called into the office to see the Section Officer. My heart was in my boots and I wondered what was wrong now. He told me I had been posted to London. I was panic stricken and so many thoughts were going through my head at the same time. The words didn't sink in. He repeated what he had said, and I told him I didn't want the posting. He only smiled and said, the matter was out of his hands. I had two days to get cleared. I went back to the workshop in a daze. Pat wanted to know what had been said, and when I told him he was shattered.

Two days were not long enough to get cleared from a camp as scattered as 32 M.U. If I had to walk everywhere I don't think I would have made it in the time. I was glad I had my bike. I left it on camp for Pat to use after I left. Clearing camp was simply a matter of getting various documents signed. These signatures meant that I had handed in all I had drawn from stores in the workshop, that Pay Accounts had paid me up to date, no charge sheet was pending, etc, etc, including F.F.I. I was then issued with a railway warrant to take me to my destination, and papers to say that I was clear at St Athan and I was taking the posting for whatever vacancy I was going to.

To say that Pat was upset at my leaving was putting it

mildly. We didn't know when we would see each other again. I told him I would write as soon as I could. I think the fact that London was being bombed so heavily at the time gave him fears for my well-being. It wasn't easy to say goodbye to him.

I set off on the journey to my London posting. This time I was completely on my own. I had to make my way to a place called Kidbrooke in south-east London and report to No. 1 Balloon Centre. The work I would be doing was a mystery. I was told that I would be working at a Battery Clinic, but that meant nothing to me.

On my arrival I went through the usual preliminaries and found to my amazement, that my posting was for No. 1 M.U. which was just down the road. I was only attached to No. 1 Balloon Centre for my food and accommodation. My billet was a long hut similar to the one at Innsworth. There was about two dozen girls there altogether and they all work at the M.U. Most of them were Charging Board Operators (C.B.O.s) and they had been trained to know all there was to know about all types of batteries. There were a couple of clerks and myself. Two more electricians joined us later.

The girls were split up into three different groups and each group worked a different shift, keeping a round the clock duty roster. There were about six C.B.O.s to a shift and one W.A.A.F. and one R.A.F. electrician. The men were billeted out in civvy digs.

The work carried out at the Battery Clinic was more of an experiment and very confidential – so we were told. The section was responsible for collecting all unserviceable batteries from dozens of small R.A.F. units scattered in and around London. These were brought into the clinic, examined and most of them were put through a special process to bring them up to a working standard. Although they were never used in aircraft again they were put back into service for "ground use only". We electricians carried out stringent tests on all processed batteries before they left the clinic, and the percentage that passed these tests was very high. Hundreds of batteries were put back into service that would otherwise have been scrapped.

Being attached to the Balloon Centre had its advantages. We couldn't do exactly as we liked but we did have it pretty easy. Being on shift work enabled us to come and go as we pleased, as no one seemed to keep track. We kept ourselves to ourselves. We were known as the "M.U. Girls" and this seemed to explain away any irregularities. I think the only persons we got to know were the N.A.A.F.I. and cook-house staff and the S.P.s (Service Police) on the gate.

I reported for work at No. 1 M.U. Although I'd learned a bit about batteries it was only theory. I'd had no practical experience. As soon as I arrived in the workshop I was met by the Flight Sergeant. He was in charge of everyone at the clinic and was responsible to the Flying Officer. If ever the phrase "his bark is worse than his bite" fitted anyone, it fitted him.

He scowled at me and asked my name and if I had ever worked on batteries before. When I told him that I hadn't, he asked me what I had done. He seemed to scowl even more when I told him. He said, nothing but passed me over to the clerk–cum–stores assistant. She gave me a lecture on protective clothing and I was issued with a pair of navy blue dungarees, a rubber apron that covered me almost to my ankles, rubber gloves and wooden soled clogs. I had to wear this lot over my battledress before I could start work! I was given a paper to read which explained the use of acid and the proper way to handle it, what to do if spilt and how to treat acid burns to the body or eyes. I began to wish that I was miles away.

I walked slowly into the workshop and I could hardly move with all the clobber on! Chiefy (Flight Sergeant) saw me and immediately shouted to me, "Empty that battery," pointing to a battery standing on the floor. I didn't know where or how to empty it. I must have looked stupid. Then he yelled, "The sink is over there." He pointed to the other side of the workshop and went on, "You pick it up, carry it over and then turn the bloody thing upside down." I was a little bit scared of him until I saw the C.B.O.s stifling a giggle. I was glad when the day was over. I took a long time to settle down at Kidbrooke and I missed Pat terribly.

We had a rest room at the Battery Clinic where we girls could change into our working clothes, shoes, etc. It was only a small room with a few lockers, a table and a couple of chairs. We also had a gas ring, kettle, saucepan and frying pan. When we were on night shift we would have a meal during the night and we would take turns to act as cook. The food was issued at No. 1 Balloon Centre Cookhouse. We never knew in advance what we would be getting and we never had any choice. The box of rations was usually collected by one of us and carried down to the workshop. Sometimes it would be sausages and mash, or beans and bacon but, whatever it was, they knew our cooking facilities were limited.

Next door to the clinic was another small workshop, which was known as the repair shop. Airmen electricians worked there repairing the batteries that needed resealing or changing a cracked case before processing. They, too, worked shifts. There were only a couple of them on each shift. Although they were all in civvy digs they would join us for the meal during the night. It was rather a rough and ready type of meal, usually eaten from a plate resting on our knees. Seating was limited but we always managed somehow. There was no music at all but sometimes we would have a singsong, especially if a raid was in progress.

I had an old gramophone at home. It was quite a modern one in those days – it didn't have a horn but it did have a handle to wind it. Although it was portable it was very heavy. I went home one weekend and brought the gramophone back to camp with me, complete with needles and one record (one of the old 78s). The record was a "selection from Chu Chin Chow". This record was later played so many times that I think it must have been almost worn through to the other side. Then we had trouble with the sound box. The aluminium-foiled piece was torn. We tried hard to repair it, but couldn't. Replacement was impossible. In the end we used a piece of silver paper to try to get it to go. It worked but we had to strain our ears to hear it. I never did know what happened to that gramophone, but I still remember the words and music of "Chu Chin Chow".

Not only did I have to get used to the work, the new environment and the girls, but also the air raids. These were really something. There was sometimes hardly any occasions at all in which to take cover and I don't think it was the bombs that were as alarming as the gunfire. The report of the guns was almost deafening and constant during a raid. The shrapnel literally rained down causing sparks to fly as it hit the ground. One night about eight of us had to make a run for the shelter during a raid, only to find it was packed solid with other W.A.A.F. personnel and there was hardly any room for us to get in. When we did we found several girls in hysterics and more in a state of collapse. I'd been in raids at home but had never seen anything like this.

Panic seemed to have spread to almost mass hysteria. This was unusual and I don't know what started it. The raid was a heavy one and overhead, so that may have been the explanation. On the whole, people, at such times, were usually very quiet and subdued no matter what their feelings. That was the only time I experienced such behaviour.

We had a lot of free time at Kidbrooke – it may have been the fact that we worked shifts and it just seemed like more time to ourselves. Every third week, when we changed from early shift to night shift, we had nearly four days off. We finished at 2pm on Friday and didn't have to report again until 10pm the following Monday. With all this time to spare it was natural for us to want to get home for a couple of days, but this was out of the question. Official passes were not that easy to come by and the only way we could get around the regularities was by changing into civilian clothes and travelling home that way. Civvies on camp were strictly forbidden but that didn't deter us while a certain amount of care had to be taken to keep them hidden. Most of us had civvies tucked away somewhere in the billet.

When my long weekend came around I would pack what I needed of my personal belongings in a small holdall and, with my suitcase full of civilian clothes I would walk to the railway station at Kidbrooke. There in the ladies' toilets I would take off my uniform and dress again in my civvies. I packed my uniform away in the suitcase and left it in the Left Luggage Office on the station. I was all set then to travel as a civilian either to home or to see Pat. On my return I would collect my suitcase from the Left Luggage Office and, this time change into my uniform, pack my civvies and then get back to camp. This was a regular performance by most of us who lived reasonably near home. By doing this I was able to see Pat every three weeks, even if he hadn't got much time off himself!

He was very fortunate in a way because he had been moved into the battery shop on 32 M.U. which was just a small workshop where all the batteries on the M.U. were charged. He worked with two more fellows on a shift rota, much the same as me. If he wanted any extra time off, one of the fellows would usually cover for him. We were able to see each other much more frequently. The only other snag we had was the cost of the railway fare. Neither of us had a great deal of money to spend and seeing each other so often drained our resources. I was told of a way to get forwards and backwards to Wales quite cheaply so this is what I did.

I travelled from Paddington to Newport in Monmouth-shire on what was a straight through train. If I bought a plat-form ticket at Paddington on my way to Newport and did the same at Newport coming back, I could then get off at each station using the platform tickets on the next trip. As long as I always had a proper ticket to show the conductor, should he want to see it, it was OK. The trains were usually heaving with servicemen and women and the conductor could rarely do his job properly, if indeed he could do it at all. I'm sure I wasn't the only one who travelled this way.

There must have been dozens who did the same thing. Only once was I caught and that was only because my proper ticket was out of date! Then I simply paid the conductor and bought a new ticket later for my next trip. Of course there were times when I went home to Ipswich. Usually I would use one of my shorter weekends for the trip because the travelling didn't take long. Being able to get home to see my family and being able to see Pat as frequently as I did was most fortunate. Life was much more pleasant for me than for a great many others who were so very far away from their loved ones. It was often too far for them to travel home even on a weekend pass.

Girls were still joining the services. My sister Kit was training to be a teleprinter operator. She had also joined the W.A.A.F. Like me she had been in a reserved occupation and found difficulty in leaving the khaki factory. My father, who was on leave at the time, went with her to the recruiting office and explained the situation to the officer in charge. He took her name and particulars and said he would see what could be done. Not long afterwards she had a letter asking her to go for a medical examination at Culver Street in Colchester. She passed that and was soon in the service with no more bother.

Meanwhile, my father had finished all his training and was now training others. He was a corporal-driving instructor at a W.A.A.F. driving school in Pwllheli. He didn't like the service at all; in fact he hated it and longed for the day when he would be back in civvy street.

The air raids were still a constant worry to my family left at home. Although they were growing up fast they were still young. Eileen was then 16 and still working in the silk factory. Marie was 11 and Michael a healthy six-year-old going to school. My mother coped the best she could with the air raids and food rationing and like hundreds of other women, did her best for each of us. Her letters to me were always cheerful and not for one minute did she complain or give me any cause to worry. Then one day, I had a letter from her that made me think again. On the face of it the letter was cheerful as usual, but I felt there was something wrong. I couldn't explain it if I tried. I made up my mind to go home that weekend.

My mother was surprised to see me but very pleased. She hadn't been at all well and was far from well then. Eileen had done her best to shop, cook, look after the younger ones and go to work as well as nurse my mother. It was a lot for someone of her tender years. We called in the doctor to see what was wrong with my mother who after examination said she had pleurisy. I felt I couldn't leave her to go back to camp so I wrote to my C.O. for some compassionate leave. I had seven days granted to me. It wasn't long but long enough to give my sister a break, and my mother was feeling better. She asked me not to let my father know or he would worry. Although compassionate leave had been granted on request it didn't mean that this was extra leave. It simply meant that I had to forfeit my next leave in lieu.

Pat was very sorry to learn that my mother had been so ill and was even more disappointed to think he had to spend his next leave on his own. He agreed that, faced with similar circumstances, he would have done the same thing, but he was disappointed just the same. As it happened things didn't work out too badly. He was able to spend a couple of days of his leave in London with me. He met some of the girls I worked with and visited the Y.M.C.A. where we frequently went for coffee.

He didn't like the air raids one bit and from then began to worry even more about my safety. As the raids were so persistent, the powers that be, had our rest room reinforced with great big steel girders. Although the room was made that much smaller it was also made that much safer. We didn't have to go to the air-raid shelter any more and the whole situation was much more convenient for working.

With all of us on shift work and living together in the same billet, it was difficult at times to sleep during the day. Those on night shift were often woken by the noise made by the other girls. This affected all of us in turn so we all tiptoed around and tried to be as quiet as we could, but there was always a certain amount of noise going on. We all complained about this from time to time. In the end a partition was built at the end of the billet, big enough to house six beds. These were used by the night shift. During their week of sleeping during the day, they would move into the partitioned part and so sleep undisturbed. This was a great improvement for all of us.

I hadn't been at Kidbrooke many months and one night when we were all getting ready for bed the 'Alert' sounded. We didn't always go to the shelter but waited to see if the raid came our way and then we'd decide. This particular night we heard the gunfire, then one almighty explosion. It was the biggest sounding bomb I had ever heard. We decided to get ourselves dressed and to go to the shelter. Then our W.A.A.F. C.O. came in – this was most unusual. I'd never known her to venture on the Balloon Centre before except for kit inspection. She came in unannounced and informally, and told us *not* to sleep on our beds that night but to sleep under them. If there was anything else to report she would come and see us again, otherwise we were to carry on. She said, she couldn't tell us any more than that.

None of us knew quite what to make of this at all. We proceeded to put out biscuits (three square mattresses that we used to place end to end along the length of our bed instead of one big one) under the framework of our beds, and crawled under for the night. Valerie in the next bed to me was terrified. She kept crying and wondering what was going to happen next. I didn't feel very confident but I tried to comfort her as best I could. Our C.O. didn't come back any more that night. Next day we were told that the bang we heard was some sort of aircraft crashing and blowing up. Later we were to learn that it was actually the first of the doodlebugs.

The doodlebugs came over frequently after that, and they travelled so fast that sometimes they were heard overhead before the siren had been sounded. They were recognised by their low monotonous drone like an aircraft and being jet propelled there was a tail of flame coming out at the back. When the engine stopped the doodlebug was ready to drop to earth. Wherever you were or whatever you were doing, it was best just to fall flat on your face until it had exploded. Continuing to keep upright, left you wide open to blast and flying debris and this could be very dangerous.

With the doodlebugs coming over so regularly day and night some of us decided to sleep in the air-raid shelter. There was a surface shelter quite near the billet, which was brick built with a flat reinforced concrete roof. It wasn't used very often. These surface shelters, although protective, weren't considered to be as safe as the dug out type, but they were safer than the billet. Inside were several bunk beds ready for such an emergency. We took our biscuits and blankets into the shelter and made up our beds. There were no lights inside so we had to take a candle or torch to see our way into bed.

One night, I couldn't sleep. I had gone to bed early because I was so tired, but there was something itching me. Valerie was reading in bed so I asked her to bring the candle over, as I wanted to see what it was that was irritating me. We were the only ones in the shelter at the time but there were about six beds made up ready to be slept in. I took my pyjama top off very gently while Val held the candle and after a while I saw it – a big flea! How I managed to catch it by candlelight I don't know, but I got it between my finger and thumb and then dare not let go for fear it would jump back on me again. Valerie was giggling at my predicament. I couldn't put it outside because I was stripped to the waist. Valerie still chortling, suggested I put it in someone else's bed! This was a brilliant idea I thought. With no more ado I lifted the covers of the next bed and popped in the flea. I slept after that with no more bother and forgot completely about the flea.

It was dinner time the next day. While we were eating our meal, Avis, a C.B.O., was saying what a restless night she had had. She went on to say that she was covered in bumps like fleabites and was quite convinced that she had been bitten. Valerie and I nearly choked. We started to laugh and told Avis about the flea I had caught, and what I did with it. I told her I didn't know whose bed I had put it

103

in. Avis didn't think it was at all funny. We didn't sleep in that particular air-raid shelter again.

Christmas was getting near and Pat and I were not at all sure if we would be able to get a pass or any time off for the holiday. I was hoping to spend my Christmas at home in Ipswich if I could. My father might be on leave as well and I hadn't seen him for a long time. Pat said, that if he was able to get away he was sure he wouldn't have time to travel far and he'd be lucky if he could even get to Monmouth so we didn't make any arrangements to see each other.

I had my Christmas at home and enjoyed the family atmosphere again. My father wasn't able to get home. I had the usual gifts, and among other things, my mother had been able to get me some elastic! It was very scarce in those days. Most of the other presents I had were items that could only be purchased with coupons. This made them doubly special to me because we didn't get clothing coupons in the W.A.A.F. I packed my case to go back to camp. I was glad I had borrowed a large one from one of the girls because I then had room to pack my gifts as well. I said goodbye to the family and wished them all a 'Happy New Year'.

On the way back to camp I stopped at the Y.M.C.A. London Bridge to get myself a sandwich and a cup of tea. I put my case down by the table and went to the counter to get served. When I returned my case had gone. I looked to see if anyone had moved it anywhere, but it had simply disappeared. I just couldn't make it out at all, as I hadn't turned my back for more than two minutes. What could I do? I felt so helpless. All my Christmas gifts were in there as well as other personal items and toiletries, some civilian undies and some of my kit. Even the case itself wasn't mine. The Y.M.C.A.

volunteers helped me look for it, but no luck. Apparently it wasn't the first case to disappear from that place. I went to London Bridge Station to go back to camp and spoke to the police there. There was nothing they could do to help but make notes in case someone should find it or even return it. I arrived back at camp feeling quite sick. The girl from whom I had borrowed the case wasn't particularly worried and told me not to be. All the girls tried hard to cheer me up. I think I was more shocked than anything. I still thought perhaps it would be found but it never was. I reported the theft to my superiors and my kit was eventually replaced. When next I went home I was able to fetch back some undies but my Christmas presents and other things were never replaced.

It was about three months later and I was on night duty when we had an air raid. The gunfire was terrific and we were all huddled in the rest room trying hard to sing. When the raid was over we all went outside to see if there had been any local damage and it was almost like daylight out there. Fires were everywhere. There was one huge fire just across the road and it looked as if the whole place was alight. Apart from being a transport depot, I believe it was a store where lots of records were filed away. Everything was so secret and hush, hush in those days that it was almost impossible to know what was what. I do think the depot was of some military importance.

There must have been hundreds of incendiaries dropped that night. Lots of them had gone into the ground and fizzled out. They were peppered about the place every two or three yards. The roads and pavements back to the billet were covered with them.

It was when we were relieved at 6am that morning I

learned that one incendiary had burned my bed! It had come through the roof onto the floor and then bounced back on to my bed, which was in the partitioned part of the billet at the time. Fortunately, we were all at work and the partition had stopped the smoke from penetrating the rest of the hut. Not only had my bed been burned but also my kit that was on the hot-water pipes drying behind my bed and my case full of civvies that was under my bed. The case and its contents was a big charred mess. In the case were the clothes I wore to go home at weekends which were not supposed to be there in the first place! Whether I would be able to claim for them I didn't know. I seemed to be fated not to have civvies on camp.

I saw my W.A.A.F. C.O. who wanted to have words with me about the kit that I had lost in the fire. I told her about my case of civvies that had also been burned. She was most understanding. I think she already knew that we had civvies on camp. She advised me to fill in a claim form and put down the civilian items that we were allowed to have, such as dressing gown, bedroom slippers and handkerchiefs. This way, she said, I would at least get some clothing coupons which would help a bit towards replacements, and I may be lucky enough to get some cash as well!

I filled in the claim form but it was either lost or bombed. Some months later, I had to fill in another to replace the first. I did eventually get recompensed with coupons and cash but it was only a fraction of the replacement cost.

W.A.A.F. personnel including N.C.O.s and Officers – 1944 – No. 1. M.U. Kidbrooke.

Chapter 9

Absent without Leave

WORKING in the clinic taught me to have a great respect for acid. It penetrates quietly and thoroughly. One tiny splash is perhaps unnoticed but, in a very short while, not only has it burned its way through your clothes but also starts to burn the skin beneath. Constantly working with the stuff meant that splashes were inevitable. The protective clothing was adequate up to a point. The rubber apron did its job but at times the acid would dribble down to the bottom and make contact with my dungarees. In the course of a day, according to whatever job was being done, the dreaded acid would not only burn a hole in the dungarees but also go on to the battledress beneath and sometimes the stockings beneath the battledress. This was a work hazard we had to watch closely. We were constantly going to stores for replacement clothing. This was O.K. while stocks lasted but, one day, I went to get some new slacks and there were none in the stores. I had to walk to my billet with my knees showing quite clearly through a large burn hole in each leg of my battledress. Next day, I went to the stores again and still there were no replacements. I wanted to go to Lewisham to take some collars to the laundry. I had to change into my best blue jacket and skirt. This was a bit much and everyone thought I was going on leave! I went to the stores again but still nothing. Meanwhile, I was still having to wear those ragged trousers to work and to walk up and down to the billet. I was getting fed up with this because the acid in them was ruining my stockings and irritating my legs. The acid was eating more and more of my slacks all the time. I had to do something. Being improperly dressed was one thing but, if this continued I would soon be indecently dressed!

The next morning I decided to take a walk with the girls to Lee Green. We stopped at the Y.M.C.A. for a coffee and sandwich. I wore my ragged battledress deliberately hoping someone would see me and report me. I really was a disgrace to the service, through no fault of my own. Anyway it worked. I was seen and reported. The W.A.A.F. C.O. called me into her office and asked me why I was walking about in such a state. I explained to her about stores not being able to get any slacks for me. She told me to get back to work. Later that day I had new slacks!

There was always some sort of joke being played on someone or other from time to time and usually it was un-expected. It wasn't always easy to know if someone was making a fool of you. Having finished my shift one day I went into the rest room to change. I had taken off my clogs but my shoes were not where I had left them. I hunted around, with the girls helping me, but those shoes seemed to have vanished into thin air. I couldn't possibly walk up the road in my acid eaten clogs. I knew someone was having me on but everyone had blank faces. In the end I had to wear my clogs or go in bare feet. I shuffled up the road to the billet and only hoped the S.P. on the gate wouldn't charge me with being improperly dressed. Luckily, he was in his little office and let us pass by looking out of the window.

Next day, when I got to work, there were my shoes just as I had left them. The girls from the other shift said they had been there all the time. There was only one person I hadn't asked and that was Chiefy – he wasn't there at the time! To this day I still don't know who hid my shoes, but I have reason to believe the culprit was Chiefy.

The doodlebugs were coming over more frequently and sometimes there would be two or three following one after the other. A lot of them were being shot down at the coast, but a lot more were getting through to London. Day or night it made no difference, they still kept coming. We always had to be ready for them. All the girls working on the M.U. had taken to always sleeping in the underground air-raid shelter. It was across the road from the Balloon Centre in the grounds of the Officers' Mess. Each night we would all walk over there, our battledresses covering our pyjamas, wearing cold cream and curlers and our tin helmets. We would carry our biscuits, blankets and whatever personal things we needed back and forth each day.

The air-raid shelter didn't have bunk beds like the brick built one but only wooden ledges along each side. The sides of the shelter were shored up with pieces of wood to stop the earth from falling in on us. The ledges were not wide enough to accommodate our bedding. We had to balance on them the best we could. The weight of our bodies usually held our bedding in place provided we didn't move too much in our sleep. We slept quite soundly and didn't worry a great deal about the air raids in the night but we were never sure what we would see when we emerged in the morning.

110

Travelling on the trains as frequently as I did, meant I used the underground quite a lot. For safety and protection from bombs and doodlebugs this was the ideal place to be, and most civilians were aware of it. The three-tier bunk beds lined the walls of most of the stations underground. They were crude but more comfortable than the concrete floor. Families would get there early in the evening to make sure of getting a place to sleep. Not only were the bunk beds filled but most of the platform as well. It was difficult at times to reach the train. The platforms were so crowded with sleeping bodies and their belongings, I sometimes had to step over them. These people seemed oblivious to the travellers around them. They would spend their time playing cards, knitting, sometimes singing and altogether behaving as if they were at home. While they were in the underground tunnels they were safe. There were hundreds of them trying to protect themselves and their young families from whatever was taking place above. Old and young alike would be there night after night. It was a common sight to those living in London at the time.

During the day the platforms were clear as if no one had been there but, a few hours later, the masses would be back. Even with this upheaval and discomfort, morale was high and no one spoke of defeat. Everyone was so sure that we were on the winning side. With people like this we just had to be.

One morning I had occasion to go into Lewisham to get some collars from the laundry. I had several lots to get for different girls and I walked as usual. I was alone. I hadn't gone very far down the road when the 'Alert' sounded and then I heard the drone of the doodlebug. As soon as its engine cut out I flung myself face down to the ground. It was just above me and I waited for the explosion. It was very close but I had no idea in which direction the explosion had occurred. When it was over I brushed myself down and carried on walking. As I neared Lewisham there seemed to be a lot of smoke everywhere. Then I realised it wasn't smoke but dust and it was in my mouth. I carried on further and couldn't believe my eyes. Everywhere was devastated – buses were upturned and bricks and glass strewn everywhere. People were running. I saw one woman with her hands over the eyes of the child she was carrying so that the child was unable to see the chaos. I still kept going like a robot. I stumbled over the bricks and debris that was lying in the road and picked my way to the laundry. The front was blown out and the roof half off, but I still carried on. I tripped over a bloodstained hat and trod on the broken glass of the window.

Inside there were a few people, some sitting and some standing. One woman had her clothes torn and a gash on her head, another was crying. I spoke to the assistant who had bloodstains on her overall and she looked dishevelled. She asked me if I was all right. I told her I had come for some collars and produced the tickets. She then apologised and asked me if I could possibly go back the next day! Not until then did I realise how stupid I had been to have even carried on let alone ask for the collars. I walked back to camp still stunned by what I had seen. The girls had already heard the news that Lewisham had been hit. They were pleased to see me back in one piece. I explained about the collars and apologised.

I went back to Lewisham again the next day and managed

to get the collars. The laundry was working as if nothing had happened. A lot of debris had been cleared but the roof still had a hole in it and windows were replaced with boards. It was clear that it would take more than a doodlebug to stop these courageous people.

John was the name of a new posting to the repair shop next door to the clinic. He was a quiet chap who didn't have a lot to say. He lived quite near the unit so he was lucky enough to get a sleeping-out pass and could go home each night. He didn't work nights so we didn't see a great deal of him. He was married and his wife was expecting their first baby. He was absent for a couple of days but we thought he was on a pass. It wasn't until he got back that he told us his wife had been taken ill with appendicitis and was in hospital. A few days later he was away again and this time we thought perhaps he had taken some compassionate leave to be near his wife. He was away for several days.

Then, one morning, I went into work and was both surprised and pleased to see John standing there reading D.R.O.s. I went up to him and slapped him gently on the back and said, "Morning John, how's your wife?"

He turned and said, very quietly, "She died yesterday." If he had slapped me, he couldn't have shaken me more. I told him how sorry I was and went into the rest room. I was almost in tears, I was so upset. The girls asked me what was wrong and I told them what had happened. We were all dreadfully sorry but there was nothing we could do for John. He was posted shortly afterwards.

His place in the repair shop, was taken by a young fellow called Frank. He was tall and fair and about 25 years old. He wasn't very talkative either but in a different way from John.

113

It was as if Frank found it hard to communicate. When he arrived at the clinic we were asked not to upset him in any way, but to humour him and try to be natural. This was a very unusual request. The only explanation we received was that Frank "had been through a lot". Nothing more was forthcoming, and this left us to think whatever we wanted to. He worked the usual shifts and came in for a meal at night just like the others. We laughed and talked as usual and gradually, as the days went by, he began to unwind. He was always very pleasant in his manner, but very nervous.

There was a dance being held in the N.A.A.F.I. at the Balloon Centre and the girls were going. They asked Frank if he would like to go. He refused at first but after some gentle persuasion he changed his mind. We didn't think he would turn up after what we had been told about him, but he did. I went to the dance later in the evening and was surprised to see him there. He asked me for a dance and I obliged. Whether it was a nervous breakdown he'd had I didn't know, but he held my hand in a grip so tight that I thought my bones would break and, as he was dancing, I could feel he was literally shaking from head to toe. I was a little bit scared but I didn't let him think there was anything wrong. The evening was really cool but, by the time we had finished dancing, the beads of sweat were running down his face. He thanked me for the dance and we walked back to the girls. I was relieved to get off the floor. I didn't dance with him again but he did dance with one or two of the other girls, and he seemed to be enjoying himself.

We spoke about him when we were back in the billet. The other girls had experienced much the same as me. Heaven knows what the poor man had been through but whatever it was, he was trying to overcome it. He was with us for a long time and his confidence seemed to return. At least we thought so. Whether he really did fully recover from whatever it was that had upset him I never did know.

It was May 1944. Pat and I had just spent a lovely weekend at Monmouth with his parents. The Wye Valley is a pretty place to be at that time of year. We were on the bus going back to Newport where we would then have to part and go our separate ways. I dreaded the thought of another goodbye. Although, we wrote to each other every day and saw each other more than most, parting was never easy.

Pat said that if we were to get married then perhaps I could get a posting back to St Athan. The service did try to keep man and wife as near to each other as possible. He asked me if I would be willing to marry him on my next long weekend. As much as I wanted to marry him I really didn't think it would be possible to get the arrangements made in the time and told him so. He told me to leave things to him; he would make enquiries and would write to let me know what he could find out.

I arrived back at camp and anxiously awaited his letter. I didn't tell a soul about our plans. I felt that if I did the whole thing would fall through. Nearly a week passed before I received the letter I had been waiting for.

We had previously decided on a Register Office marriage and, from what Pat said, this had to take place at Bridgend. He had been to the Register Office where they had given him a form which had to be completed and signed by both my parents before any wedding could take place. This was simply a consent form because I was still under 21 years old.

The date had been set for 3rd June (my father's birthday) at 10.30 in the morning. This meant I only had a couple of weeks to go before I was married. It wasn't long. Pat sent the form off to my mother with a letter asking her to sign and to forward it to my father. We weren't at all sure they would sign the form. I knew my parents were hoping we would wait until after the war before marrying. I kept my fingers crossed and hoped the paper would be returned in time for the wedding.

The next week was spent writing and receiving letters from both our families. None of Pat's relations would be able to get away for the wedding but his parents said they would like us to go there for our honeymoon – if we had one. My family would not be able to get to the wedding either and they received the news with mixed feelings. I think they were a bit surprised to think we were in such a hurry.

Another week had gone by and I still hadn't mentioned a thing to the girls at work. At last I got a letter from Pat to say he had received the consent form signed and completed. I was thankful for that. Time was running out and there were only a couple of days now to wait. Then I had a letter from Pat reminding me that he hadn't been able to buy the ring, as he didn't know which size to ask for. There was no time left to do anything else but to go and buy a wedding ring on my own. I wished then that I had confided in my colleagues. I went out and bought myself a utility wedding ring of nine carat gold. It was all I could get at such short notice. It cost me 29/11. I was beginning to hate all the secrecy. I wanted so much to tell everyone but I was still afraid some obstacle was going to stop our wedding.

The arrangements were that I should leave camp when I finished my shift at 2pm on Friday, 2nd June, change into my civvies as usual and make my way to the village of Dinas Powis just the other side of Cardiff. Pat had a workmate living there with his wife and young son and they had very kindly offered to put me up for the night. They were to meet me on my arrival.

Saturday morning – my wedding day. I was to catch an early train to Bridgend, which would stop at St Athan where Pat would be waiting with his best man. If all went well we should be at Bridgend in plenty of time for the wedding.

These arrangements all sounded straightforward enough and there seemed to be no problems at all. The girls at camp were still thinking that I was off on one of my usual trips to Wales and still had no idea of the plans we had been making to get wed.

It was Thursday the 1st of June with my nerves nearly shattered with all the tension. Then orders came through, as from 2nd June all leave and weekend passes were cancelled and all personnel were to be confined to camp. No reason was given. This really was the last straw and I was stunned for a while. Then I realised that if I was going to marry Pat on the Saturday I would have to do something.

I didn't quite know what to do but I knew I had to confide in someone. My chance came at lunchtime, the only time the whole shift was together apart from when there was an air raid. I quietly told them of the plans Pat and I had secretly been making for our wedding. They were thrilled to bits to hear the news and then they realised what a predicament I was in. They were willing to do whatever they could do to help me. I told them I was still going to try and get there in spite of the order confining us to camp. It was suggested that my Identity 1250 card and my permanent pass be left with them and handed in by them should it be necessary. There was no reason for anyone to think that I was anywhere else but on camp. I wouldn't need the passes if I was travelling in civvies. This I did and they promised to cover for me. They also said they would tell no one. I was convinced that I would never be missed.

I then took my life in my hands and had a word with Chiefy. He had been in the Air Force for a very long time and I valued his advice. He would know of any snags of which I wasn't aware. He scowled, as usual, and asked me how I thought I was going to get away with it. I told him my plans about the civvies, the pass and 1250. He wished me luck and told me to be careful. He also told me to go off duty at midday in case any of the trains were cancelled. I thanked him and he warned me that if I were caught he would know nothing! Still no one knew why all leave had been cancelled, only that the order applied to all R.A.F. units throughout the country. If this were so then Pat would be confined to camp as well. I didn't dare think about that. The only thing I could do was carry out the arrangements he had made and wait and see what happened.

I arrived at Dinas Powis with no trouble at all and was met as arranged. Pat arrived later and stayed for the evening. He had to get back to camp but, as far as he could tell, there was no reason why he shouldn't be on that train in the morning. I went to sleep hoping everything would go as planned.

I was awakened early with a hot cup of tea and two pretty rosebuds picked from the garden of the lady of the

Cpl. Bailey F.S.
1632822
Hut 6. Site. 2.
R.A.F. Wymeswold.

To whom it may concern.

I, Frederick Sidny Bailey, give
my consent to the marriage of my
daughter, Jean Dale Bailey, at
present serving as an L.A.C.W. in
the Waaf. and stationed at no. 1
M.U. Kidbrooke. London S.E.3.
home address 1, Rydal Walk, Ipswich
to L.A.C. Paterson of R.A.F.
at present stationed at no. 32.
M.U. St. Athans S. Wales, home
address 21, Glendower St. Monmouth. Mon.
           Signed   FS Bailey (Father)
       "   Eva Bailey (Mother)

Letter of consent to my marriage from both my parents.

house. I pinned them on my lapel. It was a beautiful morning and the war seemed a long way off. My clothes were only my ordinary civvies. I had no time to get coupons for any new clothes for this special event. I tried not to think about that. I had breakfast and was accompanied to the station by my host. I thanked her for her hospitality and boarded the train. I was on my way. I couldn't believe I was going to get married. This was supposed to be the most important day of my life. Pat was waiting at St Athan with his best man. We were introduced as the train moved away from the station.

Pat gave me two yellow roses for my buttonhole – he had picked them from the garden of the Sergeant's Mess as he came out of camp to catch the train.

We arrived at the Registry Office in good time and, after a wait of a couple of minutes we were ushered into the Office. We were then told we needed another witness, so the best man went out into the street and brought back a Sergeant of the Home Guard who was willing to act as a witness. We knew nothing about him only that his name was J. Mead – that's how he signed the register. The ceremony was carried out and we were married with no fuss, no photographs, no cake and no relatives.

We thanked our friend the Sergeant of the Home Guard and said goodbye. We never did see him again. The best man accompanied us as we travelled back to St Athan, where he got off, to go back to camp. Pat and I went on to Monmouth. Pat told me later that he had managed to get cover for his duties, and he wasn't due back until the next Tuesday midday, which was a relief.

There were congratulations all round at Pat's home on

our arrival. There were some telegrams too from my relatives and the girls back at camp who knew of our plans. The first one I opened was one that read "Return to your unit immediately." I thought at first someone was having a joke until I saw that it was signed by the W.A.A.F. C.O.

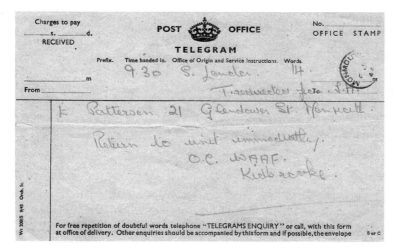

Actual telegram received on my wedding day

This was a nasty blow to both of us and shook me to my boots. How on earth did the C.O. know where I was and what had happened to make her send for me? These questions were left unanswered. After a talk with Pat and his parents I decided to stay with Pat until he went back to camp. I was in trouble anyway so I might as well be hung for a sheep as a lamb. Although Pat's parents were not in full agreement with me, they made us both very welcome while we were there.

We did not return to our respective camps until the Tuesday morning and by that time we all knew why leave had been cancelled. D–Day was the 6th June – the day we travelled back to camp. When the news broke early that morning we both thought perhaps we would have trouble getting back to our unit. It was possible that the trains could be delayed or even commandeered for troop movements but, as it happened, they were not. We both got back to camp without any incident.

As soon as I arrived at the billet I was told to report to the W.A.A.F. C.O. She charged me with being absent without leave, with no other charges. If I had gone straight back to camp after reading the telegram, I would still have been charged with the same offence, so nothing was lost. I was prepared for whatever punishment she thought fit to give to me. I was confined to camp for fourteen days with extra duties.

After the charge I was given my hat and the officer called me into her office again. This time she congratulated me on my marriage and apologised for having to punish me! She said she had to take her orders from the Adjutant.

The jankers was easy. I had no reporting to do at the guard-room and no cookhouse fatigues. I was confined to camp, and the only fatigues I did was to pick up matches and cigarette ends that had been thrown out of the billet windows, and dust the lampshades of the billet. I had nothing to do after that. I think they had run out of jobs for me. I learned later that if I had left my 'late' pass behind as well as my 1250 and permanent pass then I would never had been missed!

Pat was very fortunate. His mates covered his duties as arranged and he was never missed. In fact, when he went to the Orderly Room to change his status to 'married' on all his records they found it hard to believe that he had been married on that day. He was half expecting some sort of trouble, but nothing ever came of it. I, too, had to get my marriage on my records with my new name and signature. This all had to go through the usual channels and wasn't official until it was shown on orders.

Then, one morning at work about three weeks after we were married, the mail was delivered just as the 'Alert' was sounded. I had the usual letter from Pat and I opened it while we were in the rest room. I couldn't believe what I was reading. I read the same piece over and over again. Pat had been posted overseas. One of the girls asked me if I felt all right and offered me a seat. She thought the air raid had upset me. I couldn't speak for a while. Then I told them the news Pat had sent me. The girls were very sorry but, of course, there was nothing they or I could do. I was upset for most of that day.

The following day I received my usual letter from him. This time I didn't know whether to laugh or cry. He wrote saying he had been for his medical examination for his overseas posting and, to his utter amazement, had failed to pass. This meant he would be medically downgraded and unfit for his overseas posting. He said he had forgotten to mention he had recently got married!

Eventually my marriage was recorded on orders and I was prompted then to go ahead to try for a posting back to St Athan and, although my request was viewed very sympathetically by my C.O. I was informed that this kind of posting did take time. I lived in the hope that Pat would not be posted elsewhere before my request had time to go through the usual channels.

It was not more than a week later that four of us were walking back from Lee Green after a shopping spree (tooth-paste and soap)! when, in the distance striding towards us, I saw what I thought was a familiar figure. As he strode nearer I was more convinced that it was "Smithy" our Warrant Officer from E. & W.T. St Athan. No one had a gait quite like his! I crossed the road so that he would pass me more closely. I wanted to make sure. Yes, it was him and he recognised me too. He stopped and chatted. I would have liked to have known why he was in Kidbrooke but I felt I had no right to ask. It was so good to see him. We wished each other well and he went on his way. The chat with Smithy overwhelmed me with a longing to get back to St Athan. I didn't have long to wait.

I wasn't the only waaf from the M.U. to get married while I was at Kidbrooke. There were at least seven others who decided to take the plunge. One or two got married simply to get pregnant and so get their discharge from the service and this they openly admitted. One, whom I knew, went out of her way to get pregnant so that her boyfriend would have to marry her! One was married quickly because her boyfriend was posted overseas and the other had the usual white wedding. Whether they intended to get preg-nant or not was their affair but, usually once a girl was married the husband was never keen for her to stay in the service and pregnancy was the only way out.

Pat and I were in no hurry to start a family. The war was bad enough for adults to cope with, but with the enforced separations and never knowing what the day would bring, we began to change our outlook. Our thoughts turned to a flat in the village near St Athan – away from the bombs of

London and maybe a sleeping-out pass. We couldn't ignore the fact that this would be better than the lives we were leading at the time. No one knew for how long the war was going to last. By the time it was over we could end up being too old to have children! So I joined the rest of the wives who wanted to become pregnant but not before some of the girls at Kidbrooke had already got their discharges. Valerie was one of them.

Valerie hadn't been well for the last two weeks and we were all a little concerned about her. She said it was nothing and refused to report sick. She seemed to get over it and carried on working as usual. One evening when we were on a late shift she looked rather poorly and said she felt very ill. There was nowhere for her to lie down in the rest room so I went with her to the nearest air raid shelter on the unit. There she was able to put her feet up and rest on the wooden bench seats. She almost collapsed once and after-wards was very sick. It was about an hour later before she felt well enough to go back to work. We returned to the clinic and the girls made sure she didn't do much in the way of work. The next day she was fine and said she didn't know what had come over her. We thought no more about the incident. It was weeks later when she finally reported sick – not only was she pregnant, but she only had a month to go before her baby was due! She wasn't married and refused to tell the M.O. who the father was. She was discharged from the service. Before she left she did mention to the authorities that the father of her child was on active service in the Navy. She thought it was impossible for him to marry her before the baby was born, and that was her reason for not saying anything earlier. Within days they had flown him home and they were married. Later I was honoured by being asked to be godmother at the christening. I shared this pleasure with another waaf from the clinic. After the ceremony Valerie gave each of us one of the baby's shoes. I still have it although I have never seen Valerie or her daughter since.

Then there was Cassie who fell in love with a married airman. She really idolised him. She became pregnant but there were no wedding bells for her. Vicky was another who fell in love with a married man. They had a daughter but there was no divorce. He and Vicky are still living together as far as I know.

Chapter 10

Peace Reigns

IT was February 1945 when I was called into the office by the Section Officer. He said he was pleased to inform me that my long awaited posting to St Athan had, at last, come through. I couldn't have been more pleased. While I was sorry to have to leave all the friends I had made at Kidbrooke, I really was looking forward to the pleasure of Pat's company again. I got myself cleared at Kidbrooke and, after saying farewell to my friends, I set off again to the Land of the Bards. I didn't have to ask my way this time!

At St Athan I was booked in as usual and shown to my billet in married quarters. It was a luxury to sleep in a bed again and not to have to worry about raids. I shared a room containing three beds, one of which was unoccupied. It served the two of us as a table and a general holdall. There was also a chair.

The waaf with whom I shared the room worked in the fabric shop and her Christian name was the same as mine. She was a Welsh girl and lived in Bridgend. She was able to get home almost any time. I didn't get to know her very well as all my evenings were spent with Pat and at weekends she always went home.

When I reported for duty I had to report to the Motor Transport Section (M.T.). Once again I was going to a job where I had no previous experience. I was met by the Chiefy who was a very quietly spoken Scotsman. He showed me around the workshop and I met all the other mechanics. I was the only waaf! I hoped they weren't expecting great things from me! Then I learned there was one other R.A.F. electrician there and I began to feel much better. The workshop wasn't all that big – about the size of a small garage with a long bench the whole length of one wall and two pits. All the lorries and trucks were stood outside on a large car park. Outside the workshop and by the side of the car park was a small prefabricated building. This was where the drivers waited between jobs. The hut was divided into two separate rooms with W.A.A.F. drivers in one end and R.A.F. in the other. They would wait there until a job came up. A short distance away was another hut, which housed the office staff for the section.

After all the introductions, I was issued with navy dungarees to protect my battledress. I tried to make myself useful and walked about the workshop talking to one and then another. No one seemed very busy and when my first working day was ended I had done nothing. After a week of this I was beginning to think that I was a spare part! I began to call in at the drivers' rest room and chat with them. They were a friendly bunch of girls and seemed used to having nothing much to do. As time went on I spent more time in the rest room than I did in the workshop but I hated doing nothing. I would much rather have been kept busy. Little did I know how busy I was going to be.

Now that I was back at St Athan Pat was busy trying to find accommodation so that both of us could apply for a sleeping-out pass (S.O.P.) which would enable us to get away from the camp as soon as we had finished our work for the day. We could then see to our own catering and live similar lives to those in civvy street. In a way he was fortunate because he knew quite a few of the local inhabitants from his frequent visits to the local pubs!

This helped us a great deal when he was looking for somewhere for us to live. He finally met up with the local cobbler whose mother, an elderly lady of 78 years, had a room to let with use of kitchen and bathroom. This sounded ideal. Pat went to see her and she told him that she was perfectly willing for him to rent the room but she would like to meet me before anything was settled. I went over to see her. She was a dear old soul and very spritely for her age and we got along fine together. She told me the room was ours and we could move in as soon as we liked. We couldn't believe our luck. All we had to do now was to get permission from the C.O. This came through with no problems and within no time at all Pat and I were settled into our one room with the use of kitchen and bathroom.

Life took on a completely new look for us. We reported for duty each morning as usual, and in the evening we were able to walk home to our little place in the village. This was the village of Boverton, which is only about a mile from the camp on the road to Llantwit. In the evenings we were able to shed our uniform and change into civilian clothes and be civilians for a few hours.

I was able to do most of my shopping in the N.A.A.F.I. stores on camp, which sold nearly everything we needed so shopping was no problem. We were issued with ration cards and I had to get used to the limited supplies. It was difficult at first but, with Pat's help and suggestions, everything worked out O.K. Pat still had my old bike on camp and it came in very useful at times. We would use it to get to work if either of us were a bit late.

The old lady was very good to us and virtually gave us the run of the place. When I cooked in the evening I would cook enough for her and she rather looked forward to that. She liked to chat and would talk for hours if given the opportunity.

It was springtime and spring-cleaning was quite an event with her. I would come home in the evening to find she had washed blankets and curtains by hand. She thought nothing of it and was very methodical about the way in which she did her cleaning. She started with the room she used least of all and went through each one thoroughly until she finished in the kitchen. I helped her where and when I could. After the kitchen had been cleaned I thought she had finished, but, no, there were the outhouses to be whitewashed! She asked Pat if he would mind removing all the coal left over from the winter from her coal shed. There wasn't much to move and Pat did it for her willingly. Next day, when we came home from work, she had cleaned and whitewashed the coal shed. She then asked Pat to sift the coal and replace it, leaving the dust for her to make coal blocks! Never did I meet an old lady as hard working as she.

Meanwhile I was settling down at the workshop. There was never much to do and I made friends with Vera. I thought at first that she was a driver. She was always in the rest room. Then I asked her why she never seemed to get a driving job and she told me that she was a flight mechanic. Like me, she should have been at work in the M.T. but found so little to do that she had almost taken residence in the rest room. Vera was a S.O.P.* and lived with her parents in the village of St Athan. She wasn't married but she always had plenty of boyfriends. She used to cycle backwards and forwards to work. I think she had a compassionate posting for some reason.

As the spring days got warmer Vera and I were so bored with sitting in the rest room we asked Chiefy if we could cycle off somewhere for half an hour. He didn't mind as long as we used the back gate where there was no guard. I think he was rather relieved to be free of us for a while. He also added that if we were caught he didn't know anything about it and we would have to take the consequences. We rode to the village and back. It made a pleasant change and after that we often went out and we'd call in the tearooms in the village for toast and jam. It was the best toast I'd ever tasted! We always made sure that Chiefy was informed of our whereabouts. Work in the M.T. Section was getting more like a holiday camp.

Then, one day, we both felt like doing some work so we decided to go into the mechanics workshop to see if we could sweep up or do something. Cyril, one of the mechanics, had just finished painting the registration number and roundels on a lorry. It had taken him most of the day and he stood to admire his work. When he saw it was completely to his satisfaction he went off to find Chiefy to let him know he had finished. When he had gone I said to Vera, "I'd like to paint the whole thing over so there would be nothing for Chiefy to see."

* S.O.P. = Sleeping out pass.

131

I had no intention of doing it until Vera laughed and said, "I bet you daren't."

Without thinking twice I picked up a brush and painted out the number plate that Cyril had taken so long to do. It was a spontaneous action. Vera and I waited behind some vans to hear what might be said. Back came Cyril with Chiefy on his heels. They both stood mesmerised at the blank plates. Cyril nearly hit the roof and Chiefy simply scratched his head. Then I heard Chiefy say that the lorry driver was due to go out that night. I had no idea the job was an urgent one so thought it best to show myself and own up.

I had a serious lecture on sabotage and thought at one time that I was going to be charged. Instead, Chiefy told me the best thing I could do to make amends was to paint the numerals myself and to get them done quickly so that the lorry could go out that night. I didn't know where to start. How I managed it I don't know, but I did get the thing finished and the lorry was O.K. to go out. I wasn't very popular but nothing more was said.

The next day everyone was bright and cheerful. The dreaded lorry had gone and everyone seemed to have forgotten about it. Then Chiefy called me into his office. Once again he reproached me and I told him how sorry I was. He went on to say that, since I had made such a quick and thorough job of the painting the day before, he would like me to paint the whole fleet! Not only was I to paint the numerals and roundels but the bodywork as well. There were about a couple of dozen lorries and trucks as well as others that were out on different jobs. I thought he was joking but he wasn't. He furnished me with brushes and paint – loads of paint and all the cotton waste I would require. He told me I could start when I liked and the sooner I did, the better he'd like it. I started straight away.

The job was of no urgency so I was able to take my time. Surprisingly enough each lorry and truck didn't take as long as I had imagined it would. I had a four-inch paintbrush for the bodywork and I only had to give them one coat of a muddy green colour. The roundels and numerals I painted the day after when the green paint was dry. As fast I completed what I thought was the last one another one would book in. I thought I was never going to finish. It took me weeks. I didn't moan again about being idle.

While I was painting the trucks and lorries there were days when rain prevented me from working. On these days and sometimes when I felt like a break I would go into the rest room. There was always someone to talk to or some scandal to be talked about. On occasions I would take a walk over to E. & W.T. and speak to the girls I used to work with. They were all still there and most of them were married. Gwen was engaged. None of them had been posted. I was glad now that I hadn't spent all of my service life at St Athan. I felt the other W.A.A.F. electricians had missed something by not being posted.

Pat and I were still trying to start a family. It was taking us longer than we expected. I was beginning to think there was something wrong with me. I toyed with the idea of reporting sick and speaking to the M.O. but, somehow, this didn't appeal to me or to Pat. We kept on hoping.

One night when we were getting ready for bed there seemed to be a lot of rowdiness going on in the village somewhere. We listened and there was a lot of shouting and singing. We couldn't understand what it was. We looked out of the window but could see nothing. The noise went on for quite a while. Whatever was happening, someone was having a great time.

The next morning we went to work as usual and as we passed the square to get to the workshops we couldn't believe our eyes. There, in the middle of the parade ground, was a latrine! Neither of us could get to the workshop quick enough. We were so keen to learn what had happened.

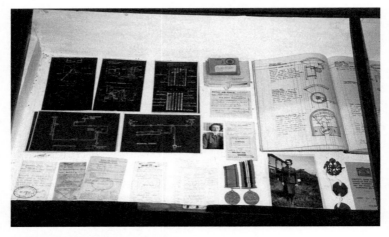

Above: Wartime memorabilia on exhibition at Norfolk and Suffolk Aviation Museum.

Looking at exhibits with an interested visitor.

Chapter 11

At last . . . Demob

NEWS had been received that the war in Europe had ceased. No wonder there had been high jinks the night before – the noise we had heard must have occurred after the news was received on camp. Now, although everyone was at work, there wasn't a lot done. We were all in limbo wanting to know how soon we would be able to return home. There was still the war in the Far East to be settled. It was going to be months before we could be discharged. We all carried on as usual but the waiting seemed to be endless.

As everyone settled down again and work was back on track the 'war effort' seemed to have lost its urgency, but the discipline still applied. Fire watching and blackout were no longer as important as they were, and rules were eased in that direction. Everything was much more relaxed but some things continued. I was still, more than ever, anxious to have a baby.

A couple of weeks later, sitting in the rest room doing nothing, as usual, an argument cropped up about the ouija board. To prove a point someone suggested we made our own ouija board. We all set to putting the alphabet on separate pieces of card. Someone produced a drinking glass from somewhere and we all sat around in wonderment.

Each of us put the index finger of our right hand on top of the glass. Then someone said, "Is anybody there?" We all screamed with laughter. It all sounded so stupid. We tried again but a little more seriously this time. The glass moved slightly and each of us was convinced someone was pushing the glass. No one could be serious so we abandoned the idea.

The next day the subject came up again and we decided to give the glass another try. This time we didn't laugh. The glass started to move and began to spell out words. Then one of the R.A.F. drivers poked his head in the door and, when he saw what was going on, he shouted, "Ask what's going to win the big race?" – to our amazement the glass seemed to come to life and moved so fast around the table that we couldn't keep up with it. The lettered cards went flying to the floor. This shook everyone and no one wanted to carry on.

It was later in the day and we were still talking about what had happened earlier, when we decided to have another go on the ouija board. We set up the alphabet and prepared ourselves. This time everyone was a bit apprehensive and much more serious. We asked, "Who is there?"

The answer came back – "Samuel."

We asked for a surname and were told to "Read the Good Book."

We asked how old he was and the answer was "ages".

We continued "Have you got a message for us?"

"Yes."

"Who is it for?"

"Jean."

"What is your message?"

By this time I was literally shaking. The message went on "Be careful of the baby, Pat cares."

By this time I was covered in goosebumps. I didn't know whether to take the message seriously or not. It was too close to me personally to brush it aside. I didn't touch the glass again as I was a bit scared.

I told Pat what had happened when we got back home to our room, and I explained about the message. He wasn't a bit impressed but called it a "load of bunkum". In a way I was still in a kind of shock. I wanted to believe it. As far as I knew I was not pregnant and, if I were so, it would be weeks before I could know for sure. Pat suggested that I drop the subject and try to forget it. If I were pregnant I would know soon enough. I didn't speak of it again but I couldn't forget it.

Not long after the ouija board message. I was smoking a cigarette and the taste was most peculiar. I put it out and lit another. That one tasted odd as well. I put it down to the brand. As the days passed I found that my food was also tasting odd. I couldn't explain it but nothing seemed to taste the same. I asked my friends if their food was all right. They told me it was my imagination. It was when I began to be sick that I realised I might be pregnant. It was as if Pat and I had been fated to wait for the peace before we could start our family.

In those days pregnancy testing was done by an internal examination and I had to wait at least a couple of months before I could approach the M.O. It was during this time that, although the fighting was still going on in the Far East, a big victory parade was being organised here at home. It was to take place in London and every section of the armed forces and all organisations, voluntary or otherwise, would be taking part. Imagine my surprise when I was told that my name had been picked among others to go to London and represent the W.A.A.F. I felt extremely honoured and couldn't wait to tell Pat. He was pleased for me but pointed out that the parade would probably be an arduous one and I was a bit wobbly when it came to standing for any length of time. I had to agree with him. Nothing would be worse than fainting on a parade as important as this one. I was very disappointed at not being able to take part in such an historic event, but I thought it best under the circumstances. I went to see the Section Officer and asked him if I could stand down. I didn't have to explain anything to him and he accepted my request readily. No doubt there were many more W.A.A.F. personnel eager to take my place at such a prestigious parade.

Meanwhile a couple of inoculations became due. I can't remember what the jabs were for, but my name was on D.R.O.s and I was told to report to the relevant clinic. I was a bit stunned at the time. I really didn't want to go through with this as I had fears for my baby, and the war was practically over. I could not see the need so I reported to the duty sergeant and explained my position. While she understood fully the way I was feeling, she told me there wasn't much she could do but she would report it.

Some days later I was summoned to appear before a medical tribunal. Again I was worried and very nervous. I was expecting to be shot at dawn or something similar!! What if they insist I take these injections and I lose the baby – surely not??? This felt much worse than being put on a charge.

I attended the meeting at the time arranged. There were

four officers, and I was quaking. I couldn't believe this incident was so important. I don't remember the questions but I only remember telling the officers my reasons for refusing to take the jabs. I was told to wait outside. It wasn't long before I was called into the office again, where they told me that I would not have to take the injections BUT – because of the uncertainty about my pregnancy I would have to report to the M.O.

The appointment to see the Medical Officer came through very quickly. In no time at all she confirmed my pregnancy. I was delighted. I was now on my way to being discharged. I couldn't wait . . .

My discharge was similar to being posted. I had to get cleared at Stores, Pay Accounts, etc. The only difference being that, this time, it was to terminate my service and not to transfer it. Again clearance. I was given a good reference as an electrician, a railway warrant to wherever I wanted to go and some cash in lieu of civilian clothes.

Once again I was a civilian. It was a pleasant thought although I didn't know quite how to feel at first. I wasn't sorry to be out of uniform but I didn't regret one single moment of those years I had spent in the service.

That very same week we learned that war had ceased in the Far East. The present emergency was over and Britain was once more at peace with the world. Soon most of the service men and women would be back home. There was so much to look forward to.

It was only a few days after my discharge when Pat heard my name called over the tannoy system to report for demobilisation. All married women were to be demobbed first but, of course, I had already left.

Now I look upon those days with a warmth that's irreplaceable. I made a lot of friends and however long I live, there will always be a place in my heart for those bad, yet good, memories, for they were the days of my youth.

Postscript

For many years I corresponded regularly with the friends I made during those stressful times.

We occasionally had reunions where we would meet and renew old memories. However, circumstances change and memories fade.

Life goes on but some things will always remain. Ask anyone who served in the 1939–1945 War.

*The Defence Medal and War Service Medal and packaging as received –
all on exhibition.*